"The stories and your frank and candid narratives, describe family situations every family experiences. I find myself curious at the aspects of ADHD that will always clash with the way of doing things in modern life. You've used your life experiences as an experiment, which is fascinating to me. So now, what's next?"

Michael J. Manos, PhD
Head of the Center for Pediatric Behavioral
Health, Pediatric Institute
Cleveland Clinic

"Joyce Kubik is at the forefront of the field of Adult ADHD Coaching. In her new memoir, she provides the personal and telling story of how she arrived at this place in her life despite the fact – or maybe because – she was identified as an adult with ADHD, herself. Kubik shares her unique story of discovery of the effects of ADHD on herself and her family, and how she transcended these difficulties and now helps others to be able to do the same."

J. Russell Ramsay, PhD
Co-Director
Adult Treatment and Research Program
Associate Professor of Clinical Psychology
in Psychiatry
University of Pennsylvania
Perelman School of Medicine

"From the first page *Unraveling ADHD* swiftly takes the reader down an intimate, often upsetting path of increasing self-awareness regarding ADHD recognition and recovery. Kubik starts with her life as a scapegoat – a smart and sassy, confused child in an alcoholic home with profound gender discrimination and emotional abuse issues – and takes us to her current life as a successful ADHD coach. Her story is inspirational, loaded with good suggestions about how to better understand and cope with ADHD, and suggests some excellent reframing tools along the way that will help those who simply fall apart during that important transition to college. Recommended for its excellent suggestions from a serious ADHD traveller who's clearly been there and done that."

Dr. Charles Parker
Neuroscience Consultant
Child & Adult Psychiatrist

"**This was a captivating book** on the struggles of a person with ADHD and how these struggles were overcome. I would recommend this book to anyone who suspects they might have ADHD, or any professional who works with people with ADHD. This is not a boring text book of information, but an absorbing story which describes ADHD struggles in moving detail, which helps the reader understand this disorder more fully."

James Shaw, PsyD
The Ohio State University
Department of Family Medicine

"**I have known people over the years** with ADHD and this book by Joyce Kubik helps me to see the world through their eyes, from the inside out, rather than the other way around. She includes her triumphs as well as her nose-dives, and they give her narrative real credibility.

"Saint Thomas Aquinas teaches us that grace builds upon nature. When we understand how we are wired, we are in a better position to accept God's grace in the changing circumstances and challenges of daily living. This book helps me to understand better the abilities that ADHD offers an individual who is grateful for life and for God's providential care."

Rev. Timothy J. O'Conner
Pastor
St. Joseph Parish

"**As a clinical psychologist** and neuropsychologist working with children and adults with ADHD, I feel this book provides insights into the daily experiences of individuals who deal with the ramifications of ADHD raising my awareness and appreciation for the frustrations as well as the positive experiences. For clinicians who treat individuals with ADHD, this book may well provide a resource to increase understanding and empathy, as well as provide a catalyst in the therapeutic work of developing an individual's tools for coping. The 'Bridge' story of how an ADHD mind works provides an experiential perspective, a leap from the complexities of neuroscience to a personal experience."

Linda A. Hartman, PhD
Clinical Psychologist

Unraveling ADHD

*How I turned my greatest deficit
into my greatest asset*

also by joyce kubik

Plan for Success: Student
ISBN 978-0-9707241-0-6

Plan for Success: Adult
ISBN 978-0-9707241-2-0

Co-Author/Contributor
365 Ways to Succeed with ADHD
Edited by Laura Dupar, PMHNP, RN, PCC
ISBN 978-0-615-52214-2

Co-Author/Contributor
365+1 Ways to Succeed with ADHD
Edited by Laura Dupar, PMHNP, RN, PCC
ISBN 978-0-615-67524-4

Unraveling ADHD

*How I turned my greatest deficit
into my greatest asset*

Joyce A. Kubik, CMC
ADHD COACH AND CERTIFIED MASTER COACH

Foreword by J.Russell Ramsay, PhD
"NONMEDICATION TREATMENTS FOR ADULT ADHD"

SENECA
ROADS
PUBLISHING

AVON LAKE OH

First edition
Unraveling ADHD: How I turned my greatest deficit into my greatest asset
ISBN 0-9707241-3-7

The examples in this book are based on the author's personal experience with ADHD, as well as her years of coaching those with Attention Deficit Hyperactivity Disorder (ADHD). This book is not intended as a substitute for psychotherapy or the medical treatment of ADHD. The reader should consult a qualified health care professional in matters relating to health, particularly with respect to any symptoms which may require diagnosis or medical attention.

www.bridgetosuccess.net
kubikja@bridgetosuccess.net

Graphic design, book design, cover design
Randy Martin, martinDESIGN 44118

dedication

To my mom,
whose strong faith and unconditional love
sustained me through my life's journey.
You will forever be in my heart.

table of contents

My mother's 90th birthday, 2011.

acknowledgments

WRITING THIS BOOK HAS BEEN A challenging and rewarding experience, but I could not have done it without the encouragement of so many.

First of all, I'm thankful that my mom has been with me through this journey. Just her presence kept me moving forward and I'd never want to let her down.

My family has been wonderful. My husband never complained about the long hours of writing because he knew the importance of this book. And my children – I can't thank them enough for believing in me and supporting my writing this book. They've been hearing about it for years and never doubted that one day I would succeed.

Thanks to the many people in my life that I met while on the road who encouraged me to write this book. They'll never know how excited I was to hear that someone wanted to read my story.

My first advisory board didn't know me, yet they supported me and provided great advice that carried me throughout my career as an ADHD coach. Thank you.

And last but not least, I owe a tremendous amount of thanks to my editor, Randy, whose expertise and professionalism created a book worthy of reading. I couldn't have done it without you.

J. Russell Ramsay, PhD

VIRTUALLY EVERYONE READING THESE words knows of the acronym ADHD. A mere twenty years ago, this would not have been the case. Today, Attention Deficit/Hyperactivity Disorder is the leading diagnosis for children's behavior and learning problems, especially with regard to performance at school.

What remains relatively unknown to most, however, are the frequency, complexity, and deleterious effects of adult ADHD.

ADHD has been around as long as there have been human brains.

Recent scientific evidence indicates that ADHD is a problem of self-regulation, a difficulty with one's ability to organize and carry out plans for which there is a long-term payoff. It is difficult for individuals with ADHD to generate motivation for a plan or task that does not produce immediate results.

"Well then," says the skeptic, "everyone must have ADHD." Not so.

"Well then," says the skeptic, again, "surely children must grow out of it by adulthood." Again, not so.

There are three common scenarios for how adults come to be diagnosed with ADHD.

1. They were diagnosed with ADHD in childhood and continue to experience persistent symptoms into adulthood.
2. They exhibited unrecognized symptoms in childhood that did not result in impairments severe enough to need treatment until reaching adulthood.
3. They exhibited unrecognized symptoms that created impairments in childhood but specialized treatment for ADHD was not sought until adulthood, though their difficulties may have been misdiagnosed when they were younger.

The difficulties associated with a lifetime of ADHD rank among the most impairing conditions encountered in outpatient clinical psychology and psychiatry. Individuals of all ages struggle to make sense of ADHD and its impact on their lives. Many people never realize that they have ADHD.

What is insidious about ADHD is that it is not a knowledge disorder. ADHD is a problem of performance or implementation of plans and behaviors that we know are to our benefit, but that are difficult to do in the present moment. The second grader with ADHD knows to raise his hand and wait to be called on before answering in class. The high school junior with ADHD knows that it is better to work on the 25-page term paper a little bit at a time to avoid being swamped at the end. Lastly, the ADHD adult knows that income taxes are due on

April 15 and that she swore last year to not wait until the last minute to organize and file.

Again.

Having faced numerous frustrations from waiting until the last minute; missing deadlines; not following through on stated plans; underperforming in school, work, or as parent or partner; individuals with ADHD often blame themselves for all of their disappointments. The only apparently logical conclusion they arrive at is that this braided cord of experiences and frustrations represents evidence of a character flaw such as laziness, low intelligence, lack of caring, disrespect for others, or a host of other character flaws. Individuals fortunate enough to undergo a competent assessment that identifies the presence of ADHD instead come to realize that these difficulties are an effect of a highly treatable condition and are not character flaws.

Understanding, however, is not enough. The combination of therapy, medication and ADHD coaching has become the preferred approach to treating ADHD.

Medication is a highly effective treatment. However, medications alone often do not produce the behavior changes that most adults with ADHD seek from treatment, particularly for those for whom ADHD may have gone unrecognized into the third or fourth decade of life, or later, in some cases. Said differently, "pills do not teach the skills."

One of the most promising areas of study over the past decade has been the role of psychosocial treatments for adult ADHD. Therapeutic approaches adapted for ADHD, namely Cognitive Behavioral Therapy (CBT), emphasize changing behaviors and attitudes to counter long-held pessimistic outlooks and to learn to consistently implement effective coping approaches in order to generate successful experiences, competencies, and strategies.

In the past fifteen years, a new field has emerged as a treatment for adult ADHD known as ADHD Coaching, which was sparked by Hallowell and Ratey's book, *Driven To Distraction*. The authors encouraged clinicians working with adults with ADHD to adopt a more active, directive approach than was customary in traditional psychotherapy models. It was suggested that adults with ADHD would benefit from the structure and guidance provided by coaches helping them organize and keep on task.

In the past several years ADHD Coaching as a profession has defined its training and credentialing practices and developed a written code of ethics. The ADHD Coaching model draws on the framework of executive- and life-coaching models and blends principles from Positive Psychology, CBT, as well as the science of ADHD.

My first interaction with Joyce Kubik happened as a result of her research on her Bridge to Success Program. Joyce's paper, published in a peer-reviewed scientific journal, represents the first outcome study of the effects of Adult ADHD coaching on a group of adults with ADHD.

Until I read Joyce's life story on the pages of *Unraveling ADHD*, I was unaware of the evolution of her ADHD coaching career. What is unique about her narrative is the role undiagnosed ADHD played in the process of forming her identity.

Joyce discovered her ADHD as an adult. By then, she had spent many years pursuing various personal goals and experiencing enough achievement that things seemed almost normal. But at the same time, she encountered enough difficulties, setbacks, and frustrations that she was filled with an indescribable sense that something was a little bit off. Once Joyce realized she had ADHD, she could look back and see how she had spent all her life, from childhood on, suffering the effects of undiagnosed ADHD.

ADHD manifests in different ways at different ages and has different effects in different settings, often creating problems in school, work, and relationships. Joyce's story shows the long reach of ADHD, both within one's personal experience and with loved ones through her role as daughter, mother, and wife.

Unraveling ADHD is about the creation of ADHD Coaching told through the life story of one of its earliest and most skilled practitioners. Joyce Kubik shares with readers the benefits of the skills and structures she created for herself as a result of dealing with her Adult ADHD and how she uses those protocols to help countless adults deal successfully with their own ADHD.

J. Russell Ramsay, PhD, is a licensed psychologist and
assistant professor of psychology in psychiatry at the
University of Pennsylvania School of Medicine
Author: "Nonmedication Treatments for Adult ADHD"

My yearbook picture, 1965.

Joyce A. Kubik

SINCE BECOMING AWARE OF MY OWN ADHD,
I've learned just how much ADHD is misunderstood. People have no idea what it means to
live with the condition – not even those who
have it. Those of us with ADHD know that we
can't focus, recall, or stay on task. We lose and
forget just about everything. We also know how
emotional we can be and that our behavior is
demoralizing at times.

But we only know that we do these things.
What we don't know is why. Why are we unable
to do what others seem to do so easily? Why do
we live our lives so confused and overwhelmed?
And, why don't we just get our act together?

As a young person, my internal measure of
self was positive. As the years went on, life's rejections made it clear I didn't have a clue how

to make life work for me. I couldn't make my parents happy. I couldn't make myself happy. Teachers saw me as a failure and encouraged me not to go to college. They seemed to be right. I struck out three times.

But I would not give up. I was determined to fulfill my life's dream to earn a degree and make something of myself. So I taught myself how to stay on track, to understand how to operate and function with my own internal signals. Then, I began to use the knowledge I gained from my personal struggles to help others learn how to operate at their own levels and thrive. I had become an ADHD Coach.

This is not a how-to book. It is a story of personal struggles to survive in a non-ADHD world. It's a story of failure upon failure upon failure. Of life experiences that led me to the conclusion that I wasn't meant to succeed no matter how smart I may have thought I was. And when it seemed that all hope was lost, it took everything I had to move forward from a life that felt like it wasn't worth living.

Unraveling ADHD is not just any story. It is my story.

I hope my story helps you understand what it's like to live with ADHD. And the effort it takes to turn your greatest deficit into your greatest asset.

Joyce Kubik
January 2013
Avon Lake OH

Sari Solden, MS, MFCC

Author: *Women With Attention Deficit Disorder*

I LOOKED AT "UNRAVELING ADHD" from two distinct perspectives: as a professional who works with adults with ADHD, and as a woman who lives with it every day. I was interested to see what insights Joyce gathered in her journey that would help adults with ADHD improve their lives.

In Joyce's story, I discovered a personal, compelling, and honest account of a woman with ADHD – from the confusion of pre-diagnosis all the way to the triumph of personal transformation. As a girl with ADHD, Joyce was easily misunderstood and overlooked because of her unusual mixture of strengths and challenges, as well as her unique perspective on the world. As an adult with ADHD, she lived an undiagnosed life full of twists and turns, from disappointments and frustrations to the exhilaration of finally being treated and understood, slowly making sense of the pieces of the puzzle that comprise a life touched by the complexities of ADHD.

Unraveling ADHD illustrates an ADHD journey from bare survival to the point at which Joyce is able to turn her hard-earned understanding into a systematized approach to help and guide others along their path. Her sheer perseverance and her determination to find answers and make a meaningful contribution in life are inspiring. The knowledge and understanding her story generates can be used by mental health and disability counselors, organizers, and coaches to gain an inside view of women with ADHD.

Additionally, Kubik's book should be especially helpful for women who are on this same journey of self-discovery. For women who experience the challenges and strengths of ADHD, Joyce's experiences will provide validation for their own experiences, instill a sense of hope in their lives, and help them to identify with others.

What you will find on the following pages represents a fully fleshed out portrayal of a real woman living a real life with ADHD. Kubik's finely drawn portrait can help professionals see beyond the diagnosis of ADHD and deep into the inner psyche of the human being who lives every day with ADHD.

Unraveling ADHD

How I turned my greatest deficit
into my greatest asset

*"Why does everyone else's life seem to run so smoothly?
I'm always rushing around frantically, driving everyone
crazy, and everything turns into a major project.
Will I ever learn?"*

chapter one

A dysfunctional family

I TOOK A DEEP BREATH AND WALKED from the garage into our front hallway. My 16-year-old daughter, Jennifer, was standing next to the bi-fold closet doors, wearing jeans, her hair up in a ponytail, still in her winter jacket. She appeared to be going somewhere. By the scowl on her face I knew she had a question I didn't want to answer. I shook the snow off my shoes and hung my coat on the hook next to the door. I managed to find my pleasant voice.

"Hi. How was school?"

That's all it took and the two of us were at it again, yelling back and forth. As was often the case, I wasn't even sure what we were arguing about.

The front door behind me flew open.

"Mom! Mom! I gotta tell you something!"

Kate was home from school, all excited and bursting to tell me a story. Her I-can't-wait-to-tell-you entrance thrust her into the middle of my argument with Jennifer. Because in our family there was nothing unusual about this, Kate simply began talking.

While Kate babbled on and Jennifer glared at me, I clenched my teeth, stood up a little taller, and turned around quickly. I glared at Kate while I tried politely to tell her that whatever she had to say was going to have to wait. She stood there in her baggy pants, gasping for air as if someone were chasing her. She was going on about some speaker she heard at school that day.

"A speaker," I thought. "That's just great."

I rolled my eyes, put my hands on my hips, looked down at her, and sighed.

"What is so important that just can't wait?"

"Well, I heard this woman at school today and I think we have a dysfunctional family."

As Kate stood there, waiting for my response, I could see she was beaming as if she had discovered the eighth wonder of the world!

For a moment my mind went blank. What did she say?

Dysfunctional?

Why did she say that?

My mind raced back and forth, searching for the right words.

The argument between Jennifer and me was over. Now it was me and Kate.

I scowled at Kate, looking straight at her with my I-know-more-than-you-do attitude. I began to yell.

"What the hell are you talking about? You can't believe everything you hear! Just who are these people anyway?"

I was about to tell her to get out when a major revelation hit me.

I couldn't move. I didn't know what to say. I stood there

looking at Kate and I could feel my face getting flushed. My mind was filled with emotional flashbacks of my growing years that were filled with guilt and anger and frustration. Exactly what I was feeling right now.

The pain and agony of something being wrong with me – that I was different or just not right – was staring me in the face once again. I was not doing okay and Kate's observation was more accurate than I knew or wanted to know.

I started to cry. All I could do was run upstairs to my room, full of shame. I could hear the pounding of Kate's frantic footsteps as she ran up after me. Quickly, I slammed the door and locked it, throwing myself onto the unmade bed, hugging the pillow as hard as I could, bawling my eyes out.

Kate was pounding frantically on the door. The last thing she wanted to do was make me cry.

"Mom, Mom, I'm so sorry! I didn't mean to get you upset. Please don't be angry with me."

Her voice sounded anxious as she broke into tears.

I said nothing. I was crying hard, full of anger. I didn't know who I was angry with but I knew I just wanted to be alone. I didn't want to talk. I felt foolish. At that moment, I didn't want to be a mom because I didn't know what to do or say. I was caught acting like a child to my child.

Being alone didn't happen. Kate, in her persistent and anxious manner, kept knocking on the door.

I crawled out of the bed, shuffled my way to the door, and stood still for a minute. I had to say something. This wasn't her fault. I opened the door gently. Kate stood there, tears rolling down her soft pale cheeks, looking remorseful. I reached out and grabbed her little chin, trying not to cry while I spoke. My voice was shaky.

"I'm not mad at you, Kate. I just don't know what to do with all my anger or with Jennifer's attitude. I'm sorry you got in the middle of this. But right now I just need to be alone for a while until I'm ready to come downstairs. Can you understand that?"

Kate nodded.

"Okay, Mom. But I feel bad. I'll just wait out here until you're ready."

I closed the door and went back to bed.

I could hear Kate slide her back down the wall. She sat and waited. In the distance, I could hear Jennifer.

"Oh, God, this is so stupid."

The slam of the door told me she had left the house.

I lay on the bed for more than an hour, crying into the pillow. I didn't know what to do or where to begin. Here I was, again, feeling that life was not worth living, but I kept going anyway. It was expected of me to keep the family together, to keep my chin up, to settle fights, to keep the peace, and above all to be the strength and the glue that held our family together.

"What a bunch of crap. When do I get to fall apart? When does someone rescue me? Probably when hell freezes over."

I kept replaying Kate's words: *"Mom, I think we have a dysfunctional family."*

The recording wouldn't stop. It played over and over.

"What am I supposed to do? I'm trying! I'm trying to be a good mom. I'm trying to be patient! If no one will listen to me, then what am I supposed to do? I hate the yelling and screaming. I hate it with a passion."

My husband and I grew up in families where yelling and screaming were part of the day. Now, here we were trying to raise teens of our own and apparently not doing much better.

I sat up, my back to the headboard, a box of tissues nearby. For sure, I didn't want our kids to grow up and be physically and mentally distant from each other. But that is exactly where they were headed, with me leading the way. I wanted them to enjoy each other and show compassion for one another. Like most people I wanted a happy family, yet we fought and argued every day and sometimes all day.

"What's stopping us?" I thought.

Even when the kids were fighting, those uneasy feelings emerged inside me, engaging me in more yelling and fighting. I desperately wanted it all to end.

Once I began feeling normal, I would usually apologize for my behavior and say that I would never blow up like that again. But I would. And I knew that meant I'd have to bury my feelings again, too. This time was no different. I curled up in bed and cried some more, until I was completely exhausted and mentally drained.

Kate was still waiting outside the door. Every now and then she very quietly asked, "You okay, Mom?"

Between my tears I would quietly squeeze out, "Yes, Kate, I'm fine."

"Are you coming out?" Kate asked softly.

Finally, with tear-filled eyes, head pounding and a heart heavy with sadness and pain, I knew it was time for one of my pep talks, so I could stop this nonsense. I got up and threw the tissues away in the bathroom, as if I were throwing away all my grown-up troubles. I was done feeling sorry for myself.

I opened the door and smiled weakly. Kate and I hugged and cried. I told her how sorry I was. I tried to assure her my crying was not her fault, and then tried to explain my actions. Soon we were talking about her day at school.

I tried to push it aside because it was so painful, but I couldn't stop thinking about being a dysfunctional family. I convinced myself that everything would be okay and that the argument with Jennifer would be forgotten.

Yet, tucked away in the back of my mind, I knew there would be a next time.

And so did Kate.

Sitting on my side porch, age 10.

chapter two

Disappointment

MY PARENTS CAME FROM DIFFERENT cultures. Mom was raised in Cleveland, Ohio, in a fairly well-to-do neighborhood near Lake Erie. Dad grew up in the mountains of West Virginia. Mom's family was blessed to have the latest and greatest household items and rarely saw hard times. Dad's life was about survival, with clearly defined roles for men and women. Mom graduated from high school. Dad had to quit in the eighth grade to work on the farm.

Mom, a 4', 11" Sicilian who stood every bit of six feet tall, had four brothers and sisters. She lived comfortably with the accompanying advantages of piano lessons, Girl Scouts, and sports. She was quite good at dancing on roller skates.

Dad, 5' 10" and lean, had 14 brothers and sisters. He was raised by two tough characters – his mom and his oldest sister. His father died in the 1918 flu epidemic. He had strong Christian values that were compromised when he went off to war in the 40s and was introduced to alcohol. Several times, Dad tried to quit drinking, but he couldn't. When he wasn't drinking he was gentle and kind. He loved to tease and have fun.

As would be expected from the disparity of their upbringings, my parents' values clashed, as they did over raising their children.

I was the fourth of five children. We were one year apart except for my brother who was two years younger than me. Because we lived in a small Cape Cod on the west side of Cleveland, we knew the meaning of sharing. The boys slept in the unfinished attic and my sister and I shared a bedroom.

We were pretty normal in that we challenged our parents every chance we got. I seemed to challenge them the most.

Every day I was in trouble because I was late, left a mess everywhere, and forgot just about everything I was told. Every day I hoped and prayed I'd get through the day without someone finding something wrong with me. This daily challenge made me feel stupid. By the end of most days, my mom had had it with me.

"Joyce, get over here. Is this your mess?"

I looked at her curiously. I didn't know what she was talking about.

"Oh! Sorry! I'll put it away. I just have to . . ."

I would start to walk away and Mom would grab me by the ear and say, "Now!"

So, I did.

Two minutes later, "Joyce Ann, get over her and clean up this mess you made in the bathroom. Now!"

"What did I do?" I asked.

She just stood there with one hand on her hip.

"Oh, that! I was going to clean that up, but I was reading my book for school."

I was looking at clothes on the floor, Band Aid wrappers in the sink, and the soap balanced on top of the five toothbrushes in the cup.

"I don't need any more of your excuses, young lady. Clean it up and don't let it happen again or you won't be going outside."

And she meant it!

I loved being outside and would do most anything to get there, even lying about doing my homework or chores.

When it was homework time, the five of us studied in the kitchen, squeezed around a tiny round table. Most nights, my brothers and I had fun shooting spitballs back and forth. Our books kept crashing to the floor and we would quickly pick them up, whispering "We're okay, I don't think she heard that."

We giggled and had a great time.

"Gotcha," my brother said.

"Did not. But this one's gonna hurt" and I snapped one with my fingers and hit him right on the forehead.

"Yeah, I . . . oops!"

Mom was standing right next to me. I said nothing, just cowered down into my seat. I recognized her body language. She had two hands on her hips. That meant we were all in trouble. It also meant to resign yourself to being judged guilty because she's on to you.

With a little assistance from my brothers yelling, "She started it," I was grounded and given extra chores to do for the rest of the week. The boys got a spanking from dad.

"Big deal. That was nothing compared to my punishment."

No one went out to play that night.

I remember fondly how we'd run to the corner of our brick street and wait for Dad to come home from work. When he started down our street, my brothers and I would jump up and down and yell.

"Here he comes. Get ready!"

We positioned ourselves for the big race. The five of us against Dad in his Ford Fairlane.

"Ready? Set?"

Dad came around the corner and we were off.

Dad always drove slowly until he got one house away. We ran with all our might knowing he was going to speed it up. And he did. Occasionally, he let us win. He would laugh heartily at us panting and gasping for air. We loved it!

As in any family where alcoholism exists, those times didn't happen often enough.

During his drinking days there were no races. He didn't get home for hours and we did our best not to be around when he finally did. Poor Mom had to endure his obnoxious ways. We hated Mom being upset and we hated her nagging at Dad for his drinking.

Dad would stagger in and I would try to sneak around him and get out the back door. In his commanding voice he said, "Where you going?"

With some apprehension I said, "Outside to play."

He stood there eyes half shut and smelling like beer.

"No you're not. I don't think your chores are done."

"I'll do them later." I was trying to get out of the house before the fighting started.

"No, you'll do them now."

I looked at Mom. She raised an eyebrow and nodded her head. I knew what that meant, so I stomped my feet as I left the room to do my chores. As soon as I was done, I would run out the front door.

Mom worked tirelessly to understand my erratic behavior. Dad saw me as defiant and a challenge to his authority. When he said it was time to go to bed, all five of us did exactly that. But, I always had one more question, which prompted Dad to look over his glasses and glare at me. Then he looked at my mom, which meant she was to take over and get me to bed.

I simply said, "Okay, okay, I'm going."

When Mom tried to get me to focus and listen, she did so by grabbing my chin firmly and pulling my face in front of hers.

"Look at me when I'm talking to you."

While I was looking straight into her eyes, my mind was thinking about my friends playing outside. Thoughts of their playing kickball, hurry up, and maybe I'll sneak a piece of that candy over there, were just a few of the things running through my head.

After the lecture and before letting go of my chin, Mom said, "Did you hear me?"

My eyes would dart off as I said, "Yes, can I go play now?"

She would let go of my chin and wave me off. This sort of interaction happened nearly every day. In later years, it became obvious to me that my mom had enormous amounts of patience.

The women's rights movement in the late 50s and 60s nearly did my dad in. Along with women working to support their families and obtaining an education, teens had more freedom than ever before. The Beatles were the rage, along with hippies, flower power, and wild and crazy guitar music. I loved it all! But, Dad's faith forbade music and dance. For that reason, my first dance was the prom. However, I couldn't resist singing and wiggling at the dinner table to a tune going on in my head. This didn't go over very well, and if I didn't pay attention, Dad would take a swing and I would wind up on the floor. There was never a warning.

Even though Mom tried to balance Dad's expectations of what girls should be, I was resentful because boys still had far more freedom. They could get in trouble and it was considered normal. The problem was that I preferred boys' activities over boring household chores and cooking. Something I still try to avoid. My relationship with Dad was always tense. He did seem to like my tomboyish ways when his family visited, but pleasing him any other time just didn't happen.

"Dad, I got an A on my spelling paper."

His monotone response said it all. "That's nice."

"Dad, I finished cleaning my room, can I go outside?"

He would look up and say, "What are you asking me for? Ask your mother."

One time, I was excited because I was chosen to be in the school musical.

Mom hugged me and said, "I know you'll do well."

But all I got from Dad was, "We'll see about that."

My heart sank and I had that sick feeling in my stomach. I said nothing. I thought for sure he would ruin that, too. After all, he made my sister quit Girl Scouts because she had housework to do. But Mom came through and I was allowed to sing in the school musical. Of course, Dad never came to the play, but Mom was there. I was thankful for her support.

Something that pleased Mom was my love for reading. I simply couldn't get enough. Every week the bookmobile came to our elementary school. I would do all my chores just so I could get new library books. I walked as fast as I could until I was out of sight of the house. Then I ran the last block and a half.

I would stand in line thinking, *"I hope those kids in front of me don't take all the books."*

Once I was in, I pulled at least ten books off the shelves, checked them out, and hurried home. I showed Mom every book. Then she'd asked me to read to her. While she made her delicious spaghetti sauce, I'd sit on the wobbly bench with my books stacked at the end and started reading. I'd glance up often to see Mom's approving smile.

"You're going to be a great teacher someday. I'm so proud of you."

It was her kind words that sustained me throughout the day.

To get away from the negative atmosphere at home on the weekends, I found refuge in the stables in Cleveland Metroparks. The people there were happy to see me. I'd ride my bike or walk five miles to get there. I'd park my bike in a pile of hay alongside the stables and run in to see what I could do.

"Yay! Joyce is here. We sure can use your help today. We have a couple of horses to walk and brush down. Then you can help in the stalls if you have time."

I was all smiles and happy to do it.

"Can I ride Sugarbush?"

Sugarbush was my favorite horse. He was gentle, with a beautiful shiny brown coat, and every time I came around he would nudge me with his nose.

"You sure can."

Only positive things happened at the stables. They liked my work and no one cared that I was a girl.

By the time I was in the seventh and eighth grades, my self-confidence was seriously damaged. My grades were falling to C's and D's. Mom was perplexed and disappointed that I didn't like to read anymore.

"What's going on? You can do better than this."

I felt awful. I hated school and I hated homework. Why did I have to get As and B's anyway?

I got the school-is-important lecture while I stood there rolling my eyes. I would argue until I was sent to my room crying.

"Nobody understands me. I want to pass but every time I take a quiz or test, I can't remember anything. Mom thinks I don't study, but I do. Reading just isn't fun anymore. It's just too hard."

Much later, Mom came into my room.

"Don't be so hard on yourself. You can do this. You just have to apply yourself. You used to be such a good reader. I know if you try harder, you'll do just fine."

But it never happened.

For my eighth grade history test I studied with Mom and felt prepared. When the test was passed out, I took one look at the first question and panicked. Thoughts started racing through my head. I repeated them over and over.

"What are they talking about? I never read anything about that! I'm so stupid. I don't care if I fail. This is ridiculous."

My stomach started feeling sick. All I wanted to do was cry. Then I would get angry. I couldn't think straight. I gave up and with two large swipes of the pen I made a big fat X on the test paper and turned it in.

"I'm in trouble now."

School and testing continued like this through my senior year. Despite what appeared to be poor effort, I graduated from high school in 1965. Mom smiled with pride and surely some relief. Dad merely said "uh huh" from around the corner of his newspaper.

"Thanks, Dad."

Graduating didn't feel so good anymore.

Despite the things that happened between us, I loved Dad very much. He was still drinking between occasional failed efforts to quit. It was no surprise that my parents' arguments were about his drinking, money, and him doing his part around the house. When Dad didn't want to talk about these things any longer, I became the topic.

"You just don't listen, do you. Just like when I told you not to cut Joyce's long hair and you did it anyway."

That's all he had to say and if Mom could have spoken Italian, both the arms and words would have been flying. She was finally brought to tears.

About the age of 20, I knew it was time for me to move out for Mom's sake. It was February, 1967. I was washing the dinner dishes and Mom and Dad were sitting at the kitchen table. They began to argue. I felt my body tense up and I wanted to cry. My mind was searching for ways to keep quiet, hoping it would end soon. My heart was racing. I wanted to scream but I kept my composure.

All I could think was, *"I have to get out of here. But where will I go? I can't take it anymore. I just want them to be quiet."*

I dropped the pan from my soapy hands and turned around to face them.

"I can't take this fighting any more. I'm moving out so you'll both be happier."

I don't remember what Mom said, but Dad just turned, looked at her and said, "Talk some sense into her."

I left and went to my room crying. I felt I didn't belong. I'd overstayed my welcome.

The reason I moved out was to make Mom's life easier, but Dad started blaming her for how I turned out – a single woman living on her own. This was hard, not only for my parents, but my siblings didn't know what to make of it, either. And no one was talking.

Within a few days, I found a place to live, packed my car and left. Mom didn't blame me for wanting to leave and she eventually supported my decision. Dad's ego was wounded and from that day forward he stopped talking to me, or even acknowledging my presence. His parting words to me were, "the door only swings one way."

I had no choice. This was something I had to do.

Later, when I would go home to visit, Dad would be in his usual place sitting on the sofa closest to the window reading his newspaper. One time, I brought my date, Sonny, home to meet my parents, forewarning him that my dad was not exactly my best friend. Sonny didn't think anything of it and just shrugged his shoulders. He was about 5' 8", with nicely combed black hair, and was wearing a white T-shirt and plaid shorts. We had just gone to play putt-putt.

"Hi, Dad," I said timidly.

Dad rolled his eyes upward, looked at me, looked at Sonny, and went back to reading his newspaper. I sighed with some embarrassment.

"Dad, I want you to meet Sonny."

Sonny extended his hand. Dad never looked up from his newspaper or offered a greeting of any sort.

How could Dad reject Sonny? He didn't do anything to him.

I was both angry and embarrassed for Sonny. Sonny

dropped his hand and I motioned to him to follow me into the living room to meet my mom.

Meeting Mom was a much warmer experience.

"Come in here and sit down and talk for a little bit before you leave."

We walked into the kitchen and sat down. Mom was easy to talk to, which made us forget what had just happened in the living room. We talked and laughed for a while and Mom offered us something to drink. But we had plans and needed to leave.

Needless to say, I never brought anyone home again when Dad was there.

Even when I was by myself, visiting Mom when Dad was home was very awkward. As soon as I walked in the door, I could feel the tension. I tried not to be as bull-headed as he was, so I said "Hi" every time I visited. But Dad maintained his silence.

Mom and I would start to talk but being ignored became so uncomfortable that we simply went into the kitchen to talk, leaving Dad to stew in the living room with his newspaper. This went on for many years.

After much contemplation, I made the decision to end the five-year marathon of Dad not talking to me. I had caused Mom enough grief.

One Saturday, I came home to visit and found my dad resting on the couch. My mom was working.

"Hi, Dad."

There was no reaction. He wouldn't even look up. My heart was pounding in my throat.

"I can't stand seeing Mom hurt. She did nothing wrong. Whatever made you stop talking to me was my fault, not hers."

He still didn't look up. Then, in a quivering voice, I told him something that finally got a response.

"It's okay if you hate me, Dad. You don't even have to love me. I just don't want Mom to be so stressed and hurt every time

I come over. She doesn't deserve it. I'm asking you to stop taking things out on Mom every time she does something for me."

Dad turned quickly toward me, and with a surprised look and a raised voice he said, "I don't hate you!"

"But you haven't spoken to me in five years," I said.

"It's not because I don't love you. You wouldn't get off the phone when I told you to. You were so stubborn and defiant."

I scowled at him and shook my head.

"Five years?"

Then I remembered how he hated the telephone. I recalled the day he was yelling because he wanted to rip it out of the wall. I couldn't believe his reason for not talking to me for five years was over a telephone and my differences. We continued our talk and by the time we were through, Dad had agreed to treat Mom better.

The next day Mom called to ask what had happened.

"I've never seen your dad cry."

"Really, Mom?" I said with raised brows. I couldn't believe he cried.

"I told him that he didn't have to love me, but it mattered more to me that he start treating you better."

She was so surprised and we both cried. We spoke a while longer and I had some hope that things would get better for Mom. And, they did.

My memory is not all that clear about those difficult times. My mother's memory always was. So, when she was 90 years old, I decided to ask her how she felt when I came home for a visit and Dad wouldn't talk to me.

I went to her cozy two-bedroom apartment on the west side of Cleveland. She began with a deep sigh and some exasperation in her voice.

"I never understood how he could treat you that way, especially when you were the only one who would sit by his side whenever he was sick from drinking. Everyone else was outside playing. You always worried about him and tried to comfort him."

"Did it bother you when we had to move to the kitchen to talk?"

Without hesitation she shook her head firmly.

"Not one bit! I was always glad to see you and talk with you because I worried so much. And, your dad was not going to stop me from talking to you. He couldn't do that. It took me awhile to understand that you had to move out and find your way. It just wasn't something young ladies did in our day and I had to work through that. What you did hurt him and he never understood it."

Those were difficult days in my life. Having the courage to face it alone was not easy. As with so many things, time heals all wounds. But it would be some time before my dad and I would have what you might call a normal relationship.

My brothers and sister, 1954.

chapter three

Just not smart enough

MY FIRST JOB OUT OF HIGH SCHOOL involved typing addresses on envelopes. Could anything be more boring?

"This is ridiculous," I thought. *"I can't even get up and walk around until it's official break time. I feel like a caged animal."*

After three days I quit.

I continued with office jobs, each one teaching me different skills, as well as the meaning of office politics. Because I became easily bored with each and every job I had, over the next ten years, I changed jobs nine times. I had to come up with an excuse every time I quit, since the look on my mom's face always said, "Are you ever going to settle down?"

Mom was especially disappointed when I left my job with Household Finance. It was there that I met my best friend, Jane, in 1966. We did all the clerical work and pretty much anything they asked us to do, including making phone calls in collections. I liked those phone calls the best. I could pretend I was an agent, a neighbor, or an old friend just to get information on the whereabouts of people. It was exciting and different every day. But then the rules changed and we weren't allowed to make those calls.

While talking with Jane recently, she recalled that "The atmosphere in the office was a bit unusual just as the people were, including us. There was the complainer, the comedian, the guy with the greasy hairdo and pointed shoes, the young and easily irritated just-out-of-high school girl we called 'Noches,' and the two wisecrackers, you and me. We all had a great time laughing or doing some silly antics throughout the day. It was a fun job with fun people."

So when I quit, Mom was upset.

"I don't understand, Joyce. You were doing so well and making enough money to pay your bills and rent. What happened?"

"I don't know. I just got bored. I needed to do something else."

"What is 'something else'?" she asked. "Do you even have a job lined up?"

"I have my application in at the IRS and that's going to go through real soon." I used my best authoritative voice so it would sound like I knew just what I was doing.

Mom sighed.

"I sure hope you know what you're doing. Next time you want to leave a job, why don't you just talk to me first?"

"Alright, I can do that."

I just wanted to appease her. Had I said anything else I would have heard a much longer lecture.

What I really wanted was to be an executive secretary and Household Finance did not offer that position. I then realized that it would take a better education to get a really good secretarial job. I broached the subject with my parents. Mom smiled pleasantly but didn't say anything. Dad, from behind his newspaper, calmly told me the same thing he'd told my sister.

"Girls don't need to go to college to raise a family. Boys go to college. But if you do try to go, don't look at me for any help."

That was that, and I knew better than to disagree with him, even though I did.

Even though I wasn't going to college, my girlfriends still asked what I was going to do. I smiled.

"I don't really want to go to college. I'm alright being a secretary."

I'd disappointed myself before with poor decisions, like putting a big fat X on a history test, but this felt different. It was a sadness I had never felt before. Not understanding my sorrow, I put it out of my mind for many years.

Then, I started to think seriously about going to college. My sister earned her nursing degree while working at a hamburger stand at the end of the street. If she could do that, I guessed I could earn mine while working in offices.

In 1966 I signed up for a couple of intro courses at a community college in Cleveland. The first night, I learned that lots of girls go to college. Filled with excitement about my new journey, I worked hard at my studies. However, it quickly began to feel like being back in high school. I couldn't concentrate and when it came to doing homework I had no motivation. I got further and further behind and started to worry that college was not for me. I didn't want to believe it so I dropped out in the first semester and dismissed it as not being ready for college. Mom agreed and nothing more was said.

My second attempt in 1968 didn't go well either, even though I met with the community college advisor who thought being a little older made me more ready for college.

We decided I'd take only two classes. At the registration desk I breathed deeply, and told myself, *"It'll be OK. I'm just starting off easy to see how it goes. I know I'm smart enough, I just have to apply myself as mom said."*

I recalled briefly, my first try at college. I was certain that over the past couple of years, I had matured and was surely ready. My stomach churned when I signed the registration for algebra and a medical science class. This would take care of my math requirement, my most difficult subject and one I barely passed in high school.

But maturity didn't help one bit.

I opened that algebra book and my stomach flip flopped. I read the instructions over and over in order to find the mystery number "x" but none of it stuck in my head. It made sense when the professor explained it, but not when I tried to do it. It was as if I hadn't even heard him.

With my hand on my head I thought, *"I don't know how I'm going to do this. It's too confusing."*

Many evenings, I would sit at the table, just staring at the page. I couldn't move forward.

"I'm so stupid," would play over and over in my head, until I slammed the book shut and tears began rolling down my cheeks.

"What was I thinking? Algebra!" I shouted. "I must be crazy to think I could do this."

I started pacing the floor, and decided that maybe the next day my head would be clearer. This went on for weeks. I didn't want to ask the professor for help because that would probably end up just like asking for help in high school. The teacher would explain the lesson, it would make sense to me, and then when I'd tried to do it by myself I wouldn't be able to make it happen. It seemed hopeless.

The medical science course wasn't much better. I often questioned the point of studying because I would read the assignment and not retain any of it. When the professor called on me it appeared I wasn't prepared. It wasn't true, but I had no idea how to explain my problem. I asked Mom about it.

"Maybe there's too much noise where you are studying. Do you have the TV on?"

Feeling a little frustration coming on I looked right at her.

"I need it, Mom. It's my background noise."

I'm sure this was déjà vu for her, but her voice remained calm.

"Maybe you should try studying without it. You just might learn more. Are you going out too much and not studying enough? What about sleep? Are you getting enough?"

"I don't know. Maybe. I just feel so different from the others. Maybe I just don't have what it takes to go to college."

My voice began to escalate and I was talking faster.

"I don't even know what I was thinking when I made this decision. I wasn't the smartest kid in high school and now trying to go to college is just proving how true that is. I'm so upset! I just don't have what it takes. Dad was right. College isn't for me, I'm just a girl."

Mom took a deep breath.

"That's not true, Joyce. You're very smart. I know high school was hard for you but that doesn't mean you can't succeed in college. You have to figure this out. I know you can do this."

I looked away.

"I don't want to talk about this anymore."

But Mom wasn't done with me yet. She leaned forward and spoke to me in her tone of voice that meant, "Stick around, there's more to come".

"Remember when you were about 10 or 12 and you put on all those plays in the neighborhood?"

I rolled my eyes.

"What does that have to do with college?"

"You would go to the library and find plays to put on with everyone in the neighborhood. You organized all the parts, memorized your lines, and you and the other kids performed in one of the garages for all the parents and kids. Not just anyone can do that. It was a lot of planning and organizing. You were the director and everyone had so much fun. All the parents loved it and you were always so happy doing it. And what about the Mission Circle you and Jackie started? That was another great thing you did, raising money to send to the missions. You have what it takes to go to college. You just have to work at it. Study more. Get help!"

Tears welled up in my eyes at the same time anger rose in my voice.

"I don't want to talk about this anymore. I'm not like everyone else. I'm different. I shouldn't have wasted money I didn't have."

I returned to my apartment, disappointed in myself and angry because I had let Mom down. It was the second time I had failed college. I curled up in a ball on the floor and cried.

"Why can't I do this, Lord? It doesn't seem fair. My mind is so messed up and I hate it! I don't want to see anyone again, especially my family. I can't bear to see their faces and hear them make excuses for my stupidity. They must think telling me it's no big deal, or that I don't need college to be a secretary makes it easier. It doesn't."

The more I thought about it the angrier I got.

"Why the drive for that degree anyway? A stupid piece of paper that says I went to college, therefore I am smart! Big deal! How many idiots do you know with college degrees? I'm smarter than so many of the people I work with."

I grew silent and began to calm down. Then I whispered.

"But I still want that degree."

I couldn't hold my eyes open any longer and I drifted off to sleep.

The next day I went through the motions of getting myself off to another boring day at work. If people asked about school I'd just say, "I did okay but I'm not going back right away".

It was eight years before I made a third attempt. In 1976, I chose John Carroll University, a more prestigious college where all the smart kids went. I figured I would do better there and was excited about the prospects. My attitude was better and I'd matured. I went out and bought all new notebooks, book bag, pencils and binders. I couldn't wait.

For summer session, I took Composition Rhetoric, chiefly because I'd been writing and journaling for many years. It was an exciting semester and I was doing well and felt energized. Professor Berry, who had traveled all over the world writing non-fiction books about her adventures, left a lasting impression.

"What a great thing to do. I'd surely like to write and get published."

I worked hard in her class and earned an A. The professor was taken with my writing and asked me to submit one of my articles to Reader's Digest. She felt it would be a good fit for the publication.

"You really think it's that good? Thank you, I'll think about it."

I was stunned. But, I kept putting off the idea of submitting the article long enough for my thoughts to once again turn negative.

"This won't get published. I can't believe my work is that good. The professor was probably just trying to be nice to me."

Mom was excited about the possibility that her daughter could get published. But even her excitement didn't change my mind.

I kept thinking, *"What if I submit it and it's rejected? That's all I need. Then I'd be the laughing stock once again."*

I ripped up the article and threw it away.

One thing that helped me to continue the next semester was the A I had earned in composition. I took history and sociology courses. I enjoyed both classes but couldn't pass a test for my life. I knew the answers but couldn't get them from my head to the paper. And participating in class was difficult because I could never find the words I wanted to say.

I sighed and shook my head.

"Here I go again. What's wrong with me? I tried going for help, but even help didn't help. I couldn't believe this was happening again. I thought for sure I would make it this time."

But I didn't. Frustrated, I withdrew from both classes. I dropped the idea of ever returning to college and told my mom and anyone else that it was just too expensive. I'd stick to clerical work and save my money.

In reality, I was heartbroken.

I really wanted that college degree.

Family outing, 1984

chapter four

Breaking point

OVER TIME MY RELATIONSHIP with Dad grew stronger and although he wasn't able to embrace it 100 hundred percent, he was trying. In September, 1976, Jim and I were engaged. Since Dad knew nothing about me and Jim, he was caught off guard.

"You don't know what you're doing."

With a deep breath I said, "Dad, I'm very happy with Jim and . . . ."

Mom gave me a look so stern, I stopped talking in mid-sentence. She motioned to Jim and me.

"Let's go into the family room and talk about things."

She knew Dad wouldn't follow. It took a few months for Dad to realize that Jim was going to be part of the family. Eventually, Dad warmed up and our conversations became more relaxed.

Jim and I were married in September, 1977, and moved to LaGrange, Ohio, where we built a colonial home that sat on a half acre in the midst of farm country. With a golf course behind us, we were entertained well into the evening by the sounds of frogs and other critters.

One of the things that Jim and I had in common was that we both appreciated making things from scratch. He loved working with wood and built almost everything in our home – tables, cabinets, pantry, benches, and many beautiful architectural touches. Before our son was born I enjoyed being his helper in his workshop, as well as painting and decorating our home. I enjoyed sewing and all kinds of crafts. I made curtains and drapes and clothes. And when I didn't understand a pattern, I could always count on Jim to get me through. We enjoyed our quiet life in rural Ohio and getting our home ready to welcome our family yet to come.

While our lives seemed quite normal, I began to notice some of my early childhood emotions coming back. I recalled how I was admonished continually for being the last one ready and making everyone late. I couldn't seem to get out the door without running around, as my mother would say, "like a chicken with your head cut off." I never understood why I couldn't get ready as the others did.

I would tell my mom, "I can't help it. I had to find my shoes, or my gloves, or whatever."

Mom would grab me and send me out the door without whatever I was looking for, telling me, "You were to be ready by now. I told you earlier we had to leave, so just get in the car as you are."

Of course, that just opened it up for my brothers and sister to express their feelings about the situation. Before I knew it, everyone was fighting because I wasn't ready. With four of us in the back seat, we had some interesting yelling matches. I think my mom wore out the phrase, "don't make me come back there" because we heard it just about every day.

On the inside, I was a very sensitive child. On the outside, I was a real toughie. I fought to protect myself from the daily criticism of being told I was late, wrong, or in trouble. I was an emotional wreck, feeling guilty for not being what my parents expected me to be. My days were spent looking over my shoulder to see who was next to catch me doing something wrong. Many nights I lay awake wondering why no one liked me or why everyone thought I was so dumb. I tried to think of ways to be more like everyone so I wouldn't get in trouble, but nothing seemed to work.

When I lived on my own, there was no opportunity for anyone in my family to correct me or criticize me. I was perfectly content, answering only to myself. If I made a mistake, I simply fixed it and nothing was said. If I was late for an appointment or an event, I made my apologies and told myself it would never happen again. And if it did, I just made another apology.

Once I was married, the feeling that someone was watching me closely returned.

"Why do I care? I'm married and we're supposed to share our feelings and emotions. This is something I simply have to adjust to."

But was it right that I should be feeling as if my childhood insecurities had returned? It was uncomfortable keeping that feeling inside, thinking no one could help me. I tried to tell myself I simply had to grow up.

By 1982 we had three children ages four, two, and an infant. Major events had taken place in our lives starting with my sister dying from Hodgkin's disease at 35, followed by Dad's death from cancer seven months later, on our son's second birthday.

"I can't believe he did this. After all we had been through, how could he die on our son's birthday? It's not right."

At the same time, thinking more rationally, I knew that

no one chooses their time of death. My thoughts were thrown back to all the unanswered questions about my dad, despite the hard work I'd done to try to put all that behind me. Robert Anderson, author of the long running play, *I Never Sang For My Father*, said it best.

"Death ends a life, but it does not end a relationship which continues on in the mind of the survivor, seeking a resolution it may never find."

That's exactly how I felt.

After my sister's and father's deaths, I spent many days complaining, yelling, and crying myself to sleep. I tried to pull myself out of my frazzled condition by using a skill I learned from a church workshop on being positive. Upon each day's awakening, I stood in front of the mirror and with conviction said, "I feel good. Today's going to be a great day! I'm not going to let anything get me down and I promise, Lord, not to lose my temper."

Yet, minutes later, the frustrations and yelling began and it was beginning to take a toll on my health.

Depression wasn't something our family talked about when we were growing up. If I said anything about feeling sad or being down, my mom would say, "Chin up! You'll be fine. Try a little harder, and don't worry so much. Things will be just fine."

"Okay," I would say.

After years of hearing this, and trying harder, I could only think, *"Can't she see it's not working? Doesn't she think I try? What's wrong with me?"*

As my frustrations increased, multiple canker sores erupted on my tongue and in my mouth. I tried a number of things to get rid of them. Even Mom's "drink buttermilk" remedy didn't work. My tongue was so swollen I couldn't eat anything. I kept biting down on the sores and the pain brought me to tears. Jim suggested I go to the doctor and I snapped at him.

"He can't help me. These sores will be gone on their own in two weeks."

But this time the sores were out of control, as were my negative thoughts. Eventually, I learned that the sores were an indication of my unusually high stress levels. It was my body's way of telling me I needed help.

I was 35 years old with so much to be thankful for, yet I felt sad and lonely. I had a difficult time controlling my moods and many intrusive and unwanted thoughts kept popping into my head. Sometimes my thoughts were of people dying horrible deaths, sometimes they were about my own death. I'd cry and cry and pray for the thoughts to stop – but they wouldn't. This was too much for me to handle. I felt like a failure.

"Something is really wrong with me. But if I tell anyone, they'll think I'm crazy and I'll never see my family again."

Some nights I prayed.

"Lord, it's okay to end all this. I don't really care how but if you're ready for me, then I'm ready to be with you. It's time to end this nightmare."

One day, when the kids were napping and Jim was at work, I went into the living room and started speaking out loud.

"Why Lord? Why is this happening to me?"

My heart was pounding and my mind was racing. I could feel tears welling up inside.

"What am I going to do? I need help but there is no one. I just don't know what to do."

My voice grew louder.

"Are you even there, Lord? My mother told me you were, and I've always believed it, but I'm beginning to wonder."

I started to cry uncontrollably and I felt no hope in sight. I stood in the middle of the living room, looked up so God could see me, and started screaming.

"Where are you, God? I can't do this anymore! If this is life, then I don't want it. Can't you hear me? I don't have all that strength you seem to think I have to hang in there until you are ready for me. Something has to happen and if you don't help me by tomorrow, I'm going to do something about it. This is not living!"

Hearing my own desperate cry made my knees buckle, and

I fell to the floor exhausted. I slept very little that night, making the next day a challenge to keep up with the kids.

Still afraid to complain or even admit to my erratic behavior, I did nothing until confronted by our family physician during a routine checkup for our three children. At least it seemed routine until Dr. Namen said, "I need you to take your children out to the waiting room with Jim so I can speak to you."

My heart sank.

"Oh my gosh," I thought. *"What's wrong with my kids? What did he find?"*

I hurried and dropped the kids off with Jim. I rushed back into the room.

"What's wrong?" I asked the doctor.

"The children are fine. I'm worried about you."

"Me? I'm fine!"

I had completely forgotten about my canker sores, my inability to eat, and the lack of sleep. And, I never mentioned the ranting I had done the day before.

Calmly, he said, "I've been watching you come in here for five years and I think you may be depressed."

My mouth fell to the floor.

"Are you crazy?" I shouted. "What do I have to be depressed about? I have three healthy children, a good husband, a nice home in the country and a cute little dog. I feel fine."

He waited patiently for me to vent, and then began to talk about what it meant to be clinically depressed. Unable to hold back the tears, I knew he was right. I didn't fully understand what was happening to me, but finally with much resistance, I agreed to try an antidepressant.

On the way home, though, I could feel my face tightening, and anxiety setting in.

"I'm not so sure about this doctor that we're taking our children to. He seems to think I'm depressed. That's absurd!"

It was obvious I was getting anxious. You could see it in my face and hear it in my voice. I was very tense.

Jim remained silent all the way home. What came to me during his silence was that maybe, just maybe, this was God's answer to my cry for help.

The doctor said it would take up to seven days for the medication to take effect; but it only took two. I thought I had died and gone to heaven. I felt so happy and bubbly that it actually scared me. I was dancing all over the place and having great fun with the kids.

"How could that be? Something must be wrong. No one feels this good. Is it possible the whole world feels high like this every day? That can't be. Maybe he gave me the wrong stuff."

I decided it was best to call my doctor.

"Dr. Namen, this is Joyce. I'm not sure you gave me the right medicine. This stuff makes me feel high. I never tried it, but it feels like how those kids describe taking that LSD stuff."

In retrospect, I can only imagine Dr. Namen holding the telephone far enough away so I couldn't hear him laughing. He assured me, after I read him the label, that all was okay and that I simply wasn't use to these feelings.

I thought, *"Huh, I'm okay."*

I felt stupid, and knew I owed him an apology. But Dr. Namen would not hear of it. So I continued to take the medication.

"He was right. This feeling was new to me."

All the while I was taking the antidepressant, I felt more connected to life and my family. Sadly, though, I realized I had never truly mourned my father's and my sister's deaths two years earlier. It dawned on me that I had never shed real tears and I felt like an impostor. One day, sitting in church, my loss for them washed over me as if it were yesterday. I missed them dearly and wished I had expressed my feelings more genuinely when they were alive. It was a difficult and personal loss that will stir in my heart forever.

While I believed this was the beginning of the end of my misery, there was much more to come.

With my depression under control, I felt I could do anything. The problem was, though, that I wanted to do everything that came to mind. And I wanted to do it right now!

As I continued to take my medication, I became even more unstoppable and my impatience to follow directions caused me to take twice as long to get something done. It was like the old saying, "A stitch in time saves nine," turned upside down on its head. I was late, missed appointments, and disappointed far too many people. I became concerned about this and decided to see Dr. Namen about it. I told him that I kept spiking highs and had more energy than I knew what to do with.

He asked several questions and suggested I see a psychiatrist.

"Oh my gosh!" I exclaimed. "Now what's going on?"

He wasn't sure and didn't want to say much, so I agreed to at least go and talk to the psychiatrist.

The psychiatrist, Dr. Khendel, asked a number of questions and determined that I had bipolar disorder.

"What is that?"

Dr. Khendel explained that I was cycling moods and thought that perhaps something called lithium would help.

In 1983, I added lithium to my daily medications and stayed on it for nearly ten years. During that time, Dr. Khendel and I met every couple months. I recognized that the highs and lows were under control, but something else was happening.

"Dr. Khendel," I said. "Why is it that I can't pick up a newspaper and read, 'The cafe is open until 11:00 tonight,' put it down, and tell you what I just read? The words leave my mind in seconds. I've known this about myself since I was a child, but it never occurred to me until now that it might have something to do with all this."

Dr. Khendel didn't have an answer. We had this conversation for years and eventually I stopped pursuing it, never speaking of it again.

During this time, I noticed an ad in the newspaper for Adult Children of Alcoholics (ACA). I told myself that something like that might help me find some answers to why my relationship with Dad was so rocky. Jim and I talked about it and agreed that it probably wouldn't hurt to go and see.

At the first meeting, eight people showed. We sat and talked about why we were there and about the families we grew up in. As we continued to talk, some people began to cry, some became angry.

I didn't get it, and kept thinking, *"What's the big deal? Dad drank, he was obnoxious and he made my mom sad. Didn't that happen to most people here? Hadn't they got that yet? Besides, it wasn't all the time. When dad was sober he was funny, kind, and even sensitive."*

I wanted to tell them to get over it, but something held me back.

Over the next few weeks, I listened more than I talked. I heard stories very similar to mine, and the exercises we did were thought-provoking. The conversations began to affect me but I didn't understand why. My curiosity kept growing, even though I really wasn't sure what was going on.

About the fourth week, I shared my story of how Dad treated me and Mom.

"Mom was always there for me and I felt as if she was the only one in the family who believed in me, even when she didn't understand me."

Hearing my own words I thought it sounded like I was holding a grudge. It made me uncomfortable but I continued.

"My parents argued about many things and tried to hide it from us. But often I heard their arguments and they always seemed to end up being about me and the telephone, cutting my long hair, or my money situation."

Once the group determined that I was what the ACA called the *scapegoat*, it all started making sense.

I continued.

"Dad never understood me and didn't seem to want to. He expected me to live the traditional role of a girl. I wasn't supposed to ask questions. I was supposed to do as I was told. That wasn't me and he never understood that."

I continued to explain how the last five years at home had probably been the worst.

"Dad made it clear that his life would be much easier if he didn't have to deal with me every day. My independence was clearly unforgiveable. I was different than my brothers and sister and he simply couldn't control me.

His frustration with me was seen by anyone who came to the house. I'll never forget how he'd be at the dinner table and when I'd sit down, he'd get up. I felt so insignificant."

I was getting emotional and decided to quit talking.

The week's session was ending and all our stories were told. Our assignment that week was to write a letter to the alcoholic parent in our life, telling them how we felt about our relationship.

I remember thinking, *"That's not hard to do. I know exactly what I'll say."*

And so I wrote:

> Dear Dad:
> So many years have gone by since I talked to you that day in the living room. I wanted to know why you never bothered with me or talked to me. When I left I told you you didn't have to love me, just be my friend for Mom's sake. She didn't need to feel bad. You said you loved me and I could see you were hurt by what I said. But I left. I constantly wondered why you never wanted me to do well, why you never said, "I'm proud of you." I tried to do everything to please you so your fights with Mom would stop. But, I was never right or good enough. I always thought Mom was the only one who cared about me. I'm 41 now, Dad, and still struggling with these emotions, but a little differently. You and Mom had problems with your marriage because of the drinking. Rather than swallow some pride and

go to AA you and Mom bounced me back and forth to change the subject and to prolong the inevitable. You were wrong. She was right in being upset, but not in using me. She thought she could push me to be daddy's girl – his country girl. And everybody loved me. And yes, I loved everyone unconditionally. I was caught in such a "story" of emotions. I was unable to develop my own person. I was too busy pleasing. But no one was ever pleased. Especially me. Now I see a little girl who loved her parents "unconditionally". The parents didn't see that. I was a useful tool to smooth over the marriage. Am I angry? No, I'm not. But I will never – and have not ever – played the games you two did with me. I'm getting better and this time I will stay better. I don't hate you now – thirty years ago I did. I understand the problems and at times my faith has helped me through all the years and it will continue to do so. I don't like myself for trying to please you through my adult years, but time will have to heal those wounds. Actually, I did please you but you could not find the words to say so. Your daughter, Joyce. (written 1988)

It was good putting my thoughts on paper. I meant every word. I felt strong inside. I was in control.

The next meeting each of us was asked to read our letters out loud. I smiled.

"I would be happy to read my letter."

But I was not prepared for what was about to happen.

As I started reading the letter, I felt this uneasy feeling come over me. I was choking up. The tears started rolling down my cheeks and my voice tightened up. The members of the group came in closer.. I felt their arms around my shoulders and I started bawling my eyes out. I had no idea these emotions were wrapped up inside me. I thought I was tougher than that. I tried and tried but could not read any further, so one of the women in the group finished reading my letter for me. It was weeks before I got over all the emotions that came forth. But once they did, the intensity of relief I felt was something I never expected.

There was still one more assignment. I had to write a letter from my dad to me. This would be in response to the letter I had just written him. I was afraid to write this letter. I was afraid of crying again if I had to read it out loud.

I thought, *"I don't ever want to feel such unhappiness again."*

But I was committed. I wrote my letter just as I thought Dad would have responded. This time I cried and cried as I wrote it.

> Dear Joyce,
> I can see that you must have been hurt as a child. I chose to drink and it had an impact on you and our marriage. I'm not proud of that. You are different than the rest and I knew nothing about raising kids. I thought you knew I loved you until that day in the living room when you talked to me. I can see my actions never showed it and I know I shouldn't have taken my problems out on you and that goes for your mother also. I'm glad that you are dealing with your problem and if I could be with you again, I would ask the Lord for one more chance and help you see your way through it. Now I can only speak to your heart and tell you that I did mean it when I said I loved you.
> Love,
> Dad.

The day came and each of us read our letters. I was a nervous wreck when it was my turn to read. To my surprise, no tears came. Actually, I was quite relieved. I had read the letter slowly and calmly. I was certain taking the class was the right thing to do. The entire process made me realize how the alcohol was at the root of our family problems. It wasn't me!

Our sessions might have come to an end, but I knew our journeys were just beginning. I didn't feel alone. I had the memory of the love and support I received from everyone in those sessions. It was time to begin my personal journey. I was ready to move forward. Guilt, shame, and anger had been major parts of my life. This class gave me hope that I could make lasting changes.

As the years went by I felt more at peace about Dad. I truly hoped that in some spiritual way he felt it, too.

Junior Mission Circle, 1962

chapter five

Misdiagnosis

WE LIVED IN THE COUNTRY FOR NINE years and began missing the convenience of schools and stores being close. Our kids were four, six, and eight, and we wanted to find a home that would allow us to walk and ride bikes together on sidewalks. The final push came when, by eminent domain, an electrical substation with an irritating hum was built on the farm directly across from our home.

In 1986, we looked at Avon Lake, a city situated on Lake Erie, not far from our extended families. It was an older city of about 14,000 people.

"This is perfect, Jim. Look at all the trees and how well kept this city is. And the schools are close by."

Driving through the city, it seemed to me residents had taken great pride in living there.

"You know," I said, "Just a few miles down the road is Huntington Beach where my family, aunts and uncles, and cousins, picnicked every summer holiday. It was so much fun. If we lived here, it would only take 15 minutes to drive the kids to the park."

That August we moved to a quiet cul-de-sac in Avon Lake.

Once we were settled and the kids were in school, it was time for me to look for a job. Since I hadn't worked for ten years, I prepared myself for reentering the workforce by taking classes in word processing and data entry.

I found an ad in the paper for a data entry position at a bank in downtown Cleveland, but you needed experience. I sighed, shoulders slumped. *"No one will hire me. I only have three weeks experience."*

But I knew I could catch on quickly if they would give me a chance.

The interview went well and when asked about my computer experience I said I had a few months experience. I got the job.

The bank had four long rows of computers with people entering data. I watched the person next to me enter data, asking an occasional question. I had to be careful the boss didn't see me talking because if she found out I didn't have experience, I might lose my job. By the third day I was still struggling with the program, and my boss, a tall brunette in her thirties, wearing a black suit and high heels, came up behind me. I panicked as she leaned down and whispered in my ear.

"You don't have experience, do you?"

My body tensed up and I held my breath.

"No, but I can learn quickly if you help me."

"Okay, I'll help you."

Then she smiled. "You know, I did the same thing a few years ago."

I was pleasantly surprised, stared at her for a moment, and took a breath.

"Can you show me a few things?"

"Let's see how you do."

That was my introduction to the computer world.

I learned quickly and spent the next couple of years moving about from job to job gaining experience. My biggest problems in every job were getting to work on time and once there, getting to meetings on time. I had no patience for office politics and often found myself frustrated with people's inability to move forward with projects because "that's not how we do things here." On the other hand, I was a loyal employee and a hard worker. I always did my part and anyone could count on me to come up with different ways to accomplish a task.

Out of the eight jobs I had in seven years, I was fired once. I felt bad about it, but it wasn't that my work was poor. It was the same old issues I always had with jobs and with so much of my personal life – lateness, losing things, and constantly scrambling to keep up with the workload. Fortunately, my boss was kind enough to lay me off so I could collect unemployment.

That year was tough trying to find a job. Those who had college degrees were getting the good secretarial jobs. In between my job hunting, I worked on our state senator's campaign. I did this for the experience and to have an impressive item on my resume. I traveled around the counties planning events, doing introductions at events, making phone calls, walking in parades and keeping in contact with the senator. The campaign trail provided the freedom to quickly make important decisions, leaving me with a sense of accomplishment at the end of each day.

Is there a paying job like this in the business world?

In 1989 I was hired as a secretary in a chemical plant in Avon Lake. The variety of tasks and fast pace kept the job interesting and I stayed there for five years.

This was also a time in my life when I did volunteer work for a women's civic group, the Avon Lake Junior Women's Club, a member of the Ohio Federation of Women's Clubs (OFWC) and of the General Federation of Women's Clubs (GFWC). So this was an international organization that had member clubs in cities throughout the US and in other countries. During my 20 year membership, the organization was instrumental in bringing out my leadership skills and helping me to believe in myself once again. This was a welcome, yet overwhelming, feeling. Everyone seemed positive and upbeat. I had no reason to believe anyone would be negative, yet I kept waiting for something bad to happen.

At times, I flashed back to my childhood and realized the impact of so many years of negative feedback. Over time, I heard the same things again and again.

"You're just a show-off, don't brag; you think you know everything; you always have to be the big wheel; and that's a stupid idea."

I heard these statements so often I had come to believe they were true. So even with volunteer work, I was afraid of doing anything that might result in rejection.

I recall when I was 14, the girls in our neighborhood started a mission circle. We raised funds by making Thank You notes out of wall paper samples or selling tickets to the neighborhood plays we put on. The monies were sent to Sister Mary Ferdinand, a nun who used to belong to our parish but was moved to the West Indies. We'd send her $8.50 and thought we'd sent her a million. The six members fought over who was in charge and who had the best idea. Those differences nearly ended our mission circle. I remember writing a letter to Sister Mary Ferdinand about the mission circle failing, and other members saying I acted like a big wheel. Sister wrote back to me.

> "God made all of us different. We all have different virtues, personalities and temperaments. . . . Don't ruin yourself by worrying what they do. You do your best even if they lay down on the job."

Looking back on that letter today, I can see that my leadership began at a very young age. I simply wasn't able to see that.

The club women saw my ability to lead and I jumped in with both feet, volunteering to chair nearly every committee. I was club president for two years and eventually took on positions with the district and the state. My success in seeing things through was so uplifting that my depressive moods lifted significantly. I was in my glory.

ONE OF THE PROJECTS I TOOK the lead on was proposing new 'Welcome' signs to the City of Avon Lake. I was instrumental in developing a design, getting club members' input and eventual approval. I found an architect who could pull it all together. When the project was complete, photos of me by the sign were taken and printed in the newspaper. It felt good to feel accomplished.

The GFWC was observing its bicentennial and clubs around the world celebrated that year. I was encouraged by all the good feedback I received from my previous projects and signed up to help spread the word about this great organization. I designed tray liners for local restaurants, helped write the history of Avon Lake, and helped plan the big birthday party. All the dignitaries, including state representatives, were invited. It was a grand evening.

As in many cities in Ohio, Avon Lake's telephone bills were outrageous. We bordered Cuyahoga County, which is the greater Cleveland area, and used many of their services on a regular basis – physicians, emergency services, and schools. Our extended families lived there, also. Paying monthly long distance bills of $400-$800 was not unusual but there was no reasonable plan in place to give us any relief. Back then, we were locked into one phone company.

It was recommended that the women's club take on the challenge. I thought it was a very exciting project. So, without thinking, I shot my hand into the air.

"Sure," I said. "I'd like to work on that."

On the ride home that night, I started talking out loud.

"Oh, my gosh! How do I do this? Huh, I'll think of something." And I did.

With club members' help, we started advertising in the paper for people to send us their telephone bills. We worked with businesses to get funds to afford an attorney. I got citizens to help with collecting some 6,000 signatures on a formal petition. This was to get the Public Utilities Commission of Ohio to listen and help us out.

I found myself sitting in meetings with lawyers, telephone company officials, and members of the PUCO. I joined a coalition of other cities in Ohio fighting for the same cause.

I remember going through the public hearings, a long 10-hour day. At the end of the session, one of the telephone company's attorney's came up to me and stared intently at me.

"You have a good poker face, but we will win this."

And then he said something to the effect of being careful because a lot of people could get hurt.

I maintained my poker face, mostly because I was too tired to process what he said. I was also shocked at his unprofessional behavior. Was I putting on a poker face? I wouldn't know how to do that.

So I said nothing and just smiled. I can't imagine what he was thinking.

We lost the battle at the local and state levels, but then we took it to the Ohio Supreme Court. It was a tough decision for the club to make, but we had come this far and wanted to see it to the end. Although we lost at the Supreme Court level, we did succeed in getting a plan that would help a majority of residents get their phone bill down to $20 a month. This was done through negotiations with the telephone company, the PUCO, and the Coalition.

Everyone was glad it was over and happy with the results, especially my family. Four years is a long time to be tied up with one project.

During my 20 years as a clubwoman, I grew to believe in myself. It was a great feeling to know I could do anything I put my mind to. It also felt good to be recognized for my work, instead of being told what was wrong with it. I was beginning to realize how debilitating life was when you couldn't play to your strengths because everyone seemed to have a better way for you to do something.

While my club work was important to me, my family and being a mom was my first priority. The constant turmoil in our family upset me every day. We seemed to be far more intense than other families. Preparing for most anything stressed everyone out, especially trying to get out the door on time. Getting ready for any sport practice was always a stressor.

"Jenny, we have to leave for practice in 15 minutes. Make sure you have all your stuff together," I yelled up the stairs.

"James and Kate, we're getting ready to leave in 15 minutes. Find something to bring to Jenny's practice and let's get in the car."

I went back to cleaning up the kitchen from dinner, listening for the kids to come down the stairs. I heard nothing. I started shouting from the kitchen.

"Jenny, Kate, James, what are you doing? Let's get going."

Still no sound of their footsteps. I dropped everything in my hands and marched up the stairs. I stood in front of their bedroom doors with arms crossed in front of me, I spoke firmly.

"What's going on? Can't any of you hear me? It's almost time to go. Now let's get moving."

They all jumped up and Jenny began to panic.

"Oh my gosh, we're going to be late. Come on James and Kate. We have to get going."

I went downstairs and finished cleaning up and I could hear them scurrying about. I started loading the dishwasher as they came down the stairs.

"C'mon, Mom, let's go. I'm ready," yelled Jennifer.

"Okay, just get in the car. I'll be right there."

They got in the car and waited for me. I just wanted to finish the dishwasher. It would only take a minute.

A few minutes later, Jen came rushing into the house, shouting.

"Mom! What are you doing? We're going to be late."

Irritated with her reminding me, I glared at her and said, "Jen, just get in the car. I'll be right there."

She ran out the door grumbling under her breath.

I glanced up at the clock.

"Oh, crap. How did it get to be that time? Shoot!"

Quickly, I added the last glass and slammed shut the door. Once again, we were 10 minutes late. Had I not started the dishwasher we would have been okay, but I couldn't seem to stop myself. I guess it took more than a minute.

This routine went on nearly every day and our frustration levels kept rising.

Homework time wasn't much different. I seemed to have very little control over the situation. Years of arguing got to me and I lost the desire to fight the battles. No one ever said to me, "Something must be going on in your family. Ever think of seeing a doctor?"

I kept trudging through each day as if their behavior was normal. After all, two of my children were teenagers and going through hormone changes. Jenny was the middle child and we all know how difficult they can be. And besides, sooner or later they'll catch on and stop the yelling. They just have to mature a little. I remember Mom saying, "They'll out grow it."

That was good enough for me.

Another problem, which was quite humiliating, involved my inability to recall information that I needed in order to hold a conversation. No matter what the setting, I'd completely forget what I needed to say.

While at a club function, I was asked to give a project update. My reply needed to be simple.

"I called Sarah and she informed me that Don would bring the materials to the gym within 10 days. Then, our next step would be to ask four high school students to help with the layout."

Instead, I said, "I called the uh, uh, ohhh, what's her name? You know, the tall person. She works for the owner."

They all looked at me and someone said, "Karen?"

"No, no, the tall girl. She's always so nice. She was here to talk last month."

"Carrie?"

"No." I just waived my arm and said, "Oh, forget it! Anyway, Don will have the uh, uh, stuff to the gym in about 10 days. Then the high school kids would be there. Well, first we have to ask them. You know, these are the kids who are going to help with the uh floor stuff. I mean the layout!!"

All the while I'm thinking, *"You sound so stupid. Just say it. I feel so inadequate."*

This scenario didn't just happen with club functions. It happened every day in business meetings, at home trying to explain something, or just casual conversations with friends. Each time I had to stop and search for words, I could feel myself losing credibility. To say this was frustrating was an understatement.

I brought this up to Dr. Khendel but he never seemed to have a good answer. He suggested a few ideas, but either I had already tried them, or they just didn't work.

THERE WERE MANY TIMES I felt I took on the weight of our family's problems and my efforts to get help from them were met with, "I can't help you. I have to . . . ."

No matter how hard I tried, help seemed rare. One day I sat and wrote about my frustrations.

"Today is April 3rd and I'm not feeling well at all. I'm very depressed and feeling somewhat overloaded with guilt feelings and embarrassment. Embarrassment because I can't seem to speak a sentence without sounding confused, ill from Alzheimer's disease, and just plain stupid. I can't recall people's names I've known for two years or 10 years unless I can get into a quiet, uninterrupted environment so I can think and concentrate hard. I hate playing the game of "give me a clue, or you know what I'm trying to say, or where's that thing that goes up and down'" and eventually reaching such frustration that I say, "Oh, forget it!" And the one I love has been so patient, teased, and tried to help . . . The kids get frustrated and we continue to go on like nothing is wrong . . .

"I'm also feeling like I'm taking on the weight of the family's problems. When anything went wrong with dinner, table settings, tutoring classes, the van, the Chevy, the laundry, the mess on the family room floor , . . well, just about anything, the problem was mine. Comments from everyone were made that I don't plan, or I should have known something was going to happen. Then they want to know if I took my medication. How humiliating! I should have never let anyone know about my bipolar medication because it was assumed that if I were crabby, I didn't take it. I also think it became a good excuse to get the guilty party off the hook . . . My attempts to fight back and put the blame elsewhere don't work and I really don't appreciate being the scapegoat. I'm more than willing to make changes or accept help but it seems even those changes were not good enough. For example, dinner – what a trip! No meal went by without a minimum of three complaints. It's too cold, the consistency isn't just right, why is it so dry, let me give you a hint, you forgot to put the salt on the table, can't you ever get it right, there can't be anything simpler, where's my glass?, you know I hate this stuff, I'm not eating, beans and ham don't go together. . . . I know you're trying but . . . Don't they realize this destroys my desire to even eat a meal? Actually, I've been trying to stay away from the table because if I do sit down I'm the one that has to get up and down for everything . . . . Oh woe is me."

One evening in 1993, that woe took on a new dimension. Jim and I were sitting in our family room watching the TV show 20/20. The host was talking about something called Attention Deficit Hyperactivity Disorder (ADHD), and it included a young man who had the condition. I'd never heard of it, but as we continued listening, the young man's description sounded like my life – clothes everywhere, unfinished projects in every room on every floor of the house, disorganized paper work, late or missed appointments, having great difficulty with communications, and being very defensive. And this didn't happen now and then, it happened every day.

Jim and I looked wide-eyed at each other.

"That's it! That's what I have. This thing called ADHD."

We talked about it and agreed that I should talk to Dr. Khendel.

I thought, "Is it possible that what is happening to me has a name to it? That guy described me to a tee."

It was actually a little eerie. I decided that before I went to see the doctor, I would write him a letter to explain. I was so excited and there was much to tell him.

Dear Dr. Khendel:

I was watching *20/20* on Friday past and they talked about something that has me all excited . . . last Friday *20/20* had a segment on ADD (Attention Deficit Disorders) in adults. It was me 100 percent! I have often wondered about my inability to read books, pay attention to conversations without losing it, recall problems, talking without losing my thought and constantly stammering for words and the subject I'm talking about. I believe we've talked about the talking part several times, but could not put a finger on it. I believe it has to do with ADD.

For as long as I can remember, I have had difficulty reading and retaining. When I was young (and I know I don't remember that much) I read and read and read books and never got the full story out of it. Since I can't remember, I asked my mom and she confirms that it did seem to be a problem for me. But with the competition in my family, you didn't dare look bad. You'd be eaten alive! I can read the headline of a newspaper and look away and not remember word one. I've done this many times in an effort to try and concentrate and then I would be so angry and frustrated that my self-esteem would be "I'm so stupid." I still feel the same today about reading. I get so frustrated when I'm trying to read something and can't hold the thought, that I just throw it down or avoid it if I can . . . It's terribly frustrating for someone like myself who knows what they want to say that they read or saw, but is constantly distracted by the least little thing. I have tried many suggested methods of concentration. Being alone in a quiet and small room helps sometimes but it is not a sure thing . . .

Now that I think about it, my dad never read a book, he always read short articles and news items. Even my husband after hearing *20/20* is convinced ADD is my problem. He said he's never seen a person as distracted as I am and so unfocused. It's frustrating to him.

I can be talking to someone and forget who and what they were talking about and have to quickly use some trick to put things back in place. I can never remember what whole conversations are about and I don't know how I get through all the meetings I go to. Oh, yes I do – I fudge it! People politely help me recall and even then it doesn't come to me for several hours . . .

20/20 also said ADD people are very intelligent and creative people. I'll never admit to the intelligent part but I am very creative. My mind never slows down! It would be wonderful to be able to read a book or work on one thing at a time; to remember a conversation I just had or an article I just read.

Please call me . . .

I went to my appointment on time and Dr. Khendel and I went over the letter. He explained about a recent course he took on ADHD in children. He hadn't heard of adults having ADHD, but he was willing to have me try a stimulant medication.

Before the stimulant was introduced, I was weaned off lithium while continuing the antidepressant. Dr. Khendel monitored my blood levels for the next six months and we talked about the positive effects of the medication. For the first time, I was less impulsive and I could focus while reading.

"I'm so excited about reading," I told Dr. Khendel. I was sitting up on the edge of the chair, my voice filled with excitement.

"Think about all the books I can read now. It's been so long and I've missed it. I might even be able to go back to school."

Jim was surprised to see me reading book after book and the kids would look at me curiously and say, "What are you doing?"

I simply smiled and said, "Reading."

It also felt odd after 47 years, to see such a reduction in hyperactivity and impulsivity. It felt good. While it was apparent that the diagnosis of Bipolar was incorrect, it didn't seem important to talk about it. It was part of the journey to get to this point.

Even my club work became more interesting and meaningful. I was happier and felt more connected. Curiously, my friends seemed to react differently towards me. They kept talking to me beyond club work. I wasn't quite sure what to do so I kept talking. It seemed as if they felt more comfortable with me. I felt a level of friendship I couldn't feel when I was not on medication. My personal relationships were getting better each day.

The excitement of knowing that there was a name for my forgetfulness and problems with memory made me feel that so many things were not my fault. I naturally began thinking of my past and how so many things happened because of this thing called ADHD. That was not such an exciting thought and I began to question old memories.

"Would Dad and I have gotten along better? Would he have understood me and loved me more? I wasn't crazy, was I? What must have everybody thought? Is this why I couldn't keep a job for very long? What's going to happen now? Is my brain all messed up?"

These thoughts constantly interrupted me at my new job at the bank. I couldn't shake the idea that my life could have been different. I was angry and embarrassed about my past behaviors. I would leave work, looking for some sign of hope that maybe my future would be more normal.

For two weeks I left work and cried all the way home and sometimes into the evening. My family would see me crying and kept asking, "What's wrong with you?"

I couldn't even look at them. I just said, "Nothing."

Eventually my grief turned into anger and I started telling myself, "Get over it, Joyce. Everybody has problems. You have to move on."

I realized that I had to move forward in order to help myself, and at that time I had a family that needed my attention. I would take care of me later.

During this period, our family life was somewhat improved, but we still experienced many of the same behavioral problems that were present before I took medication. Everyone still had an excuse for everything – including me – and our interactions had not improved. As a matter of fact they got worse.

I felt I was falling apart and losing control, instead of embracing this ADHD. It was the daily verbal battles and the continuous struggle to be on time for work, and appointments. It seemed impossible to completely move forward. I felt as though there were huge clouds following me, hanging over my head, and when the storms hit, they hit hard. There were clouds that took all hope away from me of ever earning a degree, clouds that stopped me from feeling capable of loving, clouds that said, "try as you may, you'll fail sooner or later."

Despite my improvement with medication for ADHD, it would be years before those clouds lifted. They seemed to keep me in my place, under lock and key.

After all, they had occupied too much of my previous life to just slip away unnoticed.

Sitting on the shore of Lake Erie, writing the first draft, 2000.

chapter six

Out of control

I SAT AT THE KITCHEN TABLE nervously tapping my fingers as Kate, a sophomore, and Jennifer, a junior, were getting ready for school. I wondered how I was going to tell them they were getting tested for ADHD, and that I had ADHD.

"Do they even know what ADHD is? I'll just tell them to get right home after school because we have somewhere to go. Then later I'll tell them where we're going."

They ran down the stairs, grabbed their book bags, and headed for the front door.

"Now's your chance," I thought.

"Get home right after school. We have someplace to go."

"Where are we going?" asked Kate.

"Just get going and I'll tell you when you get home."

Jennifer grabbed her by the arm yelling, "C'mon."

And off they went to school.

It was difficult to focus at work. I had my usual workload but kept looking at the clock every hour. I leaned on the desk and put my hands over my eyes.

"How should I tell them? They'll be so upset, and I don't want to get into an argument."

I paused.

"This is going to be hard."

Finally, it was time to go home.

On the drive home, I thought of what their reactions might be. I was pretty sure that Kate, with her caring heart, would be thrilled I was doing something to help Jennifer. On the other hand, Jennifer, so argumentative and negative, would probably get angry and refuse to go.

"I'll probably have to get a rope, tie her up, and throw her in the car."

I pulled into the garage, sat for a moment, and just shook my head.

"How did it get to this point, Lord? I can't believe I'm taking our kids to a psychologist. Am I doing the right thing?"

The girls were sitting on the hallway stairs and as soon as I got my foot in the door Jennifer scowled at me.

"Where are we going, Mom? I wanna meet my friends tonight."

Kate said, "Shut up, Jen."

I set my purse and tote on the bench in the kitchen and took a deep breath.

"Well, I never told you before, but I have ADHD, and . . ."

"Oh, brother," Jennifer interrupted, "don't you know that's what kids get?"

I started to get angry, but bit my tongue, closed my eyes for a moment, and continued.

"I was diagnosed with ADHD, and my doctor said the family needs to get tested. So that's where we are going. Get in the car, please."

Kate's eyes got really big. She stood up and raised her voice.

"Oh, my God! You're taking us to a shrink? This is terrible. Everyone's going to think we're crazy!"

She started running up and down the stairs.

"Kate! Calm down! This isn't going to be what you think. We're just going to talk to the doctor and no one is going to know."

After a few minutes, Kate calmed down and stopped crying. I was shocked at her response.

Immediately after Kate's outburst, Jennifer smirked and said, "It's about time you did something for me."

Wide-eyed, I could only say, "What?"

I was surprised by her comment because she had never said a word about needing help. It felt as if she were accusing me of never helping her. I just shook my head and proceeded to the car.

Once in the car, it was a quiet 15-minute ride with Jen sitting next to me and Kate mumbling in the back seat about how embarrassing this was. Jennifer just kept chiming in.

"Oh Kate, get over it."

We tried to be on our best behavior while answering a series of questions, but it was difficult. I took things personally and felt attacked with every statement. The initial diagnosis was that Jennifer had ADD and possibly depression. The psychiatrist also suggested that Oppositional Defiant Disorder (ODD) may be a concern. He highly suspected Kate had ADHD, but was more concerned that she might have anxiety. I was told to watch for depression and anxiety in both girls. He wanted to start therapy with the girls so he could further confirm the accuracy of his diagnosis, but I wasn't ready for that.

Both girls decided to ride home in the back seat and their near silence made me feel alone.

"Great," I thought. "They're mad at me."

Jen got in one swipe.

"Well, Mom, I guess we got our intelligence from Dad."

"Jennifer," I said, "That's so unfair!"

The rest of the ride home I fought to hold back the tears.

The girls and I didn't talk much about the diagnosis, but it was obvious Jennifer took it harder than Kate, who said very little. Jennifer started pitching barbs.

"Thanks a lot, Mom. It's all your fault I have ADHD."

"I'm sorry, Jennifer, but it isn't just me. This is hereditary and I really don't think it matters who we got it from. We just have to work at this and take our medicine like the doctor said. So, please stop saying that."

She shrugged with slumped shoulders.

"Whatever, Mom."

As the weeks passed, Jennifer continued to push me to my boiling point.

"Thanks a lot, Mom. It's all your fault," she would say every time she passed me in the hallway,

Finally I grabbed her by the arm and dragged her into the dining room.

"Come here. I'll show you who's responsible for this."

I picked up the genealogy book, opened it and dropped it onto the table. Jennifer was scowling as I rolled out the pages listing family members as far back as the 1600s. I stood up tall, sternly looked her straight in the eye, and with my index finger pointed to some guy named John from the 1600s.

"There's the guy who started it. Why don't we go dig him up and ask him some questions?"

Jennifer lost the scowl on her face and didn't move.

"You're crazy!"

"Yes, I am, Jennifer, and I don't ever want to hear another word from you about where this ADHD comes from."

I rolled up the pages and slammed the book shut. She never played the blame game again.

Jennifer and I went about our lives without ever addressing the emotional battle we'd been waging. The girls and I plowed our way through each day, trying to cope with our impulsivity and emotional outbursts. I was also hyperactive, which meant that everything I did was at full speed. I didn't calmly walk through the house; I looked like I was in a race – a race to get 10 feet further in record time.

In the same sense, I was unrealistic about the time it took to complete tasks, and beat myself up trying to get too much stuff done in one day. Then, I beat myself up for not getting to the one thing that had seemed the most important to complete. I acted on everything with great urgency. Even things like gathering the cake mixes in the pantry and putting them in one spot; addressing all the birthday cards for July and August, when it was only June; or updating all the family pictures in the large frame in the family room.

With my head buzzing, I would think, *"Why does everyone else's life seem to run so smooth? I'm always frantically rushing around, driving everyone crazy, and everything turns into a major project. Will I ever learn?"*

Emotionally, I was still a wreck. If something went wrong, I went into overdrive feeling foolish or stupid, and would never forgive myself. For our 20th wedding anniversary, my husband had bought me a gold, heart-shaped locket with a leaf design etched into the case. I wore it often and had put our honeymoon photos into the case. I had only had the locket two months when our little black dog, Deon, found the locket on the stairs, in a box, in a plastic zip-locked bag. He chewed it into something nearly unrecognizable. Jim wasn't nearly as upset as I was.

"Don't worry about it," he said calmly. "I'll get you another one."

I didn't want another one. I should have taken care of the first one.

"What's wrong with me?" I yelled to Jim. "I can't seem to take care of anything. Why do you bother buying me anything nice? It just gets wrecked. I'm not supposed to have anything nice. Don't you get it? I feel awful."

My guilt plagued me for some time and I had to tell Jim once more how bad I felt. In a letter to him I said:

"I feel very strong about being a responsible person and taking responsibility for all that is in my possession. To say with such pride how much I love something and to feel in my heart that you bought that locket because it is what I wanted, and you went the distance to get it for me, and then to have it destroyed in two months, just tears my heart in two. . . . It is a pain I thought I'd never feel again. It's shame – guilt – stupid – irresponsible – unforgivable – not worthy of and not accountable for my lack of thinking about what I do. It is a pattern that is well embedded in my brain and goes back too many years to remember. The pain of being let down and rejected."

It took time and therapy for me to forgive myself. I blamed my emotional and behavioral challenges on my inability to take my medication on a regular basis. After all, forgetting was something I did naturally and with little effort.

As time went by, I became driven to learn more about ADHD and continually asked everyone questions about their moods and medications. Jennifer was never comfortable talking about any of it, especially the medication. However, I had this need to know if she could tell it was working. One thing I did recognize was that when she took her meds she was less argumentative and more attentive to what was going on around her.

But she was tired of my questions.

I was cleaning up in the kitchen on a Saturday morning and I could tell Jennifer was in a huff about something as she stood in the hallway.

"Did you take your meds yet?"

She shot back immediately and forcefully,

"Yes, Mom, I did! Why do you always think my medicine makes me better? I can still be mean when I'm on it!"

"Yeah, but you're much easier to deal with when you've taken it, which is why I don't believe that you did."

"I'm so sick of this. You think everyone needs to be on medicine for something!"

Enraged, I dropped what I was doing and followed her into the bathroom. She tried to close the door on me, but I stuck my foot in the doorway and pushed my way in. Using both hands, Jennifer shoved me backwards into the sink. I couldn't believe what she did and all I saw from that point on was the enemy.

"There's no way she's going to get away with this."

With her back to the toilet, I went after her.

To this day, Jennifer remembers thinking, "Oh no, Mom's really mad!"

I started swinging my arms and yelling at her. Jennifer was crouched down wedged between the wall and the toilet, covering her head, yelling at me to stop and that I was crazy. I hit her several times before I realized what I was doing and had to force myself to stop. I was horrified and motionless. I began to panic. Still angry and defensive, I managed to get myself to leave the bathroom. Kate was just outside the door and I never looked at her. I was too ashamed and just wanted to get away. I went straight to my bedroom.

Scared and in tears, I doubted that I could ever forgive myself.

What have I done? I prayed for calmness and I prayed for answers.

"What is happening to me? To us? We're supposed to be a family. It wasn't that long ago that Kate came home and told me we had a dysfunctional family. Now this is happening. I have to do something about this family, but what?"

The next morning I tried to tell Jennifer that it was never okay to hit her and I was sorry.

"It's okay, Mom. It was my fault."

However, I was the parent and was supposed to be in control. I knew what I had to do and made the decision to seek therapy.

I didn't go back to the first psychologist; instead I found one in the phone book.

"I doubt my parents would have approved of a psychologist. Back in the day, no one ever spoke about mental health. I'll just have to keep it quiet," I thought. *"Maybe there's something to this thing called therapy. If it will help my family, then it's what I have to do."*

I saw Dr. Hill for several months and while it was uplifting, it was also scary. I needed to understand why our family was dysfunctional and most importantly why I lashed out at my daughter with such anger. Telling Dr. Hill that story brought back every moment of pain and disappointment. She explained to me that for a brief and unfortunate moment I didn't see Jennifer as my daughter, I saw her as me and I was my dad. While my dad never hit me, he certainly felt enraged when he saw what he thought was my defiant behavior. I hadn't realized I was carrying all this baggage from childhood.

I had so much to learn. And not just about ADHD.

I began to realize that many of my emotional battles stemmed from my dad's alcoholism, something he was incapable of overcoming. Thus his reactions stemmed more from alcohol than from anything I did or didn't do.

Each session with Dr. Hill was helpful. She taught me how to be forgiving and to move forward with my life. I have been grateful to her ever since.

Dr. Hill also understood my lifelong frustration with wanting to go to college and how stupid I felt because I kept failing. She encouraged me to think about returning to college once we were at a point that she felt I was ready to try. To start with, I had to start reading about ADHD to understand its effect on my life.

The first book she recommended I read was *Women with Attention Deficit Disorder* by Sari Solden. To focus and absorb the content, I kept a journal of everything I read. Page after page, it felt as if the author had followed me throughout my life and had written a book specifically about me. She explained my guilt, shame, and anger, as well as my inability to maintain focus and complete tasks. My mind kept flashing back to memories that made me uncomfortable. On the other hand, I felt some relief knowing my behaviors were not entirely my own fault. What I was understanding for certain was that my behaviors had to change.

Jennifer's frustrations remained obvious and I didn't know what to do. Our arguments were getting worse every day and we seemed unable to break the destructive thought patterns we had developed over the years. As I read more books about ADHD, I learned of a conference in Washington, DC in the spring of 1998.

The conference was put on by the Attention Deficit Disorder Association (ADDA), and the program contained several authors whose names I recognized. Since it was only a few months away, I thought. *"If only I could get Jennifer to go. Maybe we could find something to help us and the family."*

Jim and I talked about the conference. I would try to get Jennifer to go, but if she didn't, I'd go by myself. Jennifer was now a senior and preparing for college. I believed the conference might be able to help her achieve greater success.

I was standing at the sink peeling an apple, and Jennifer was in the hallway putting homework into her book bag. Lately our relationship had been less emotional and this seemed like a good time to ask about the conference. Without looking at her, I said, "Hey, Jen."

"What, mom."

"There's a conference on ADHD in Washington, D.C. Would you like to go?"

"Really? Washington, D.C.? Would we fly?"

"Yes, are you interested?"

"Sure, I'll go!"

Immediately, I put down the apple and the peeler and started calling. Within 15 minutes I had paid for our flight and conference registrations. I told Jennifer the arrangements were made and we couldn't get our money back. I was eager to learn as much as I could, and to visit the nation's capital. Jennifer seemed even more thrilled about our trip than I was.

We arrived with much excitement and enthusiasm. The only disappointment we had was that we were going to be two weeks early for the well-known and abundant cherry blossoms that bloomed every spring.

Jen and I split up and attended the different workshops. Later in the day, we shared what we had learned. We had gained so much knowledge that my thoughts drifted back to college. Up until then, I had not told Jennifer about my hopes of returning to school. When I mentioned it, she was all for it.

"Oh, I don't know, Jen. It seems to be so much work."

I hadn't yet told her about the times I had failed.

By late afternoon the second day, we were both overwhelmed and tired. We headed to the concierge and bought tickets for a trolley tour of D.C. It was a beautiful sunny day and Jennifer and I were enjoying each other's company along with the many sites. And to top it off, the cherry blossoms bloomed early. Joyfully, I indulged in the thought that they had bloomed early just for Jen and me.

We came home with our tote bags filled with more ADHD knowledge than we knew what to do with. I felt refreshed and ready to tackle the many challenges of living with ADHD. I didn't know where I was going to start, but I knew something good had to come from the trip. It wasn't just about the multitude of life-changing things we learned, it was also about the time I had spent with Jen. It was like the opening curtain of a Broadway play, full of great hope and expectations — mixed with far-away intangible fear.

chapter seven

Failure, failure, failure

I WAS READY TO PUT EVERYTHING I learned about controlling my ADHD into action almost before our suitcases were unpacked.

"I'm so glad we went to the conference," I told Jim. "We learned so many new things about ADHD and I can't wait to get started. Jennifer and I need to learn how to stay focused instead of just jumping from one thing to another. Many speakers talked about how easy it is to get off task. We just have to be more conscious about it."

"Well, that's good. I'm glad you got something out of it. How are . . ."

I interrupted and started rambling.

"Did you know that exercise can help our brains to stay focused? And this one speaker talked about how medicine works in the brain. It was fascinating. And then there's this thing called a body double to keep you on task. You could do that, don't you think?"

Before he could answer, I continued.

"And the books! You should have seen all the books that were there. I bought a couple -- well, a few."

I talked nonstop while Jim listened patiently. When he couldn't get a word in, he merely said, "Uh huh, that's good."

I had lost him.

In some ways I was hurt that he didn't want to listen, but in retrospect I must have driven him crazy with my excitement and constant chatter.

"Oh, one more thing," I said. "I don't know how I'm going to do it, but I have to start using a planner so I can get things done. I don't see myself using a planner, but I'll give it another shot."

"I think that's an excellent idea. I know you can do it if you try." With a gentle smile he reminded me.

"There's enough of them downstairs."

I thought for a moment.

"Oh, yeah, that's right. But I bought a different one and it really looks like a good one."

It was true that I had several planners downstairs. Each time I'd buy one I would set it up to organize my unfinished tasks and projects. Despite my sincerest efforts to manage time, including taking classes in time management, success only lasted two weeks because I'd either lose the planner, or forget it even existed.

This time it felt different. I was ready to change. I put the day's tasks aside and started setting up my new planner. It looked great and I already felt organized. Then, I posted a family calendar on the refrigerator, color-coding the kid's events and tasks. I was proud of myself for setting it up so quickly. Every bone in my body felt this was going to be a great success.

With a big smile on my face, I explained the color coding to the kids and how it was going to help us become more responsible. The benefit was that I wouldn't have to remind them and be such a nag.

Their enthusiasm did not match mine.

"Looks good, Mom."

They smiled gently and knowingly. I was used to people being less enthusiastic than me, so I left it at that. After all they were teens and planning just didn't get them excited.

The effort was hit and miss for a few weeks. I kept yelling that they weren't trying hard enough. They were still late for events and I had to keep reminding them of their responsibilities.

"Mom," said Jennifer, "This is too confusing. Remember, they said at the conference to keep it simple."

I wasn't ready to hear that after all I did to set this up.

"Well, at least I tried."

I was frustrated.

My thoughts drifted back a year.

"A dysfunctional family? Could Kate have been right? What's happening to me? To us?"

All the enthusiasm I had from the conference was dwindling. I felt those grey clouds hanging over my head and the thoughts of failure returned once again.

"Why does everything have to be so difficult? And why won't these kids try? I just don't know why I bother."

Several weeks went by. We were all back to arguing and yelling.

It was obvious our negative style of communicating was not working.

Over and over, I told myself, *"This has to stop. All we do is make excuses and blame one another and it certainly doesn't show respect."*

If I tried to reason with them, they were even more frustrated. After one of many long lectures to Kate she said, "I don't want to hear anymore of your psychobabble."

"Where the heck did she learn that word?"

I closed my eyes and shook my head. There was nothing

more to say. I was stressing out and for what? I seemed to be the only one that wanted to change. I felt I was showing respect to them and I just wanted it in return. This was a time in my life when it was all I could do to keep up with the needs and wants of three children. To hell with my needs. I guess I'll get to that later. My job now was to run to the library, the bank, the post office, the food store, the doctor, school activities, and all their sports. And frankly, I was starting to enjoy it less and less.

I soon realized that not much had changed from my years as a youth. Here I was, married with three children, and still accepting broken promises. How many times did plans fail because Dad was too drunk and never got home on time for us to spend a day together as a family? How many holidays were tempered because his drinking brought on more stress, fights and tears. Was my new family any different? We didn't have the drinking, but we certainly had the disrespect for one another. And all my yelling and all my preaching – psychobabble – and all the punishment in the world could not make anyone in this family change their strong-willed opinions and their seemingly paranoid approach to family. It was a constant battle.

I remember Dr. Hill saying, "Joyce, you have to take care of yourself. Do you ever get a chance to nap for 15 or 20 minutes?"

"Really?" I said. "First of all, I'm too hyper to take a break let alone a short nap. And, since my family has never seen me take a nap, I'm sure they'll think something is wrong."

She just smiled. "I want you to give it a try. Just 15 minutes."

"Okay, I'll try."

A few days later I announced, "I'm going to take a short nap and I don't want to be disturbed."

"What's wrong," Kate asked?

Inside I chuckled.

"Nothing. I just need to take a break."

Because I always made myself available to them, seeing their hyperactive-super mom lying down brought some very different reactions. One by one they came into the room.

"Mom, are you asleep?" asked Kate.

Jen followed, "Is she really sleeping? Mom, Mom, we have a question."

My eyes were shut, and I kept breathing smooth and easy. Then they started gently poking me.

"Mom, Mom, wake up!"

I remained still, and thought about when my dad took a nap, how you didn't dare ask him if he was asleep. My kids obviously didn't see this as sleeping. It was just Mom lying down, and that meant I could still answer questions and make decisions.

I lay there fuming inside while trying to fake my deep sleep. Their reasons for interrupting were many – a phone call, I can't find something, someone took my notebook, I'm hungry, I'm going somewhere.

The last statement got my attention and I was forced to abort the nap.

I often thought of taping a note to my forehead, draped over my eyes that said, "I'm sleeping. To wake me would be a grave mistake."

But they would probably have to ask me what grave meant.

I was out of ideas but I wanted the arguing to stop. Losing the battle to keep my family together was not an option. I kept thinking about the conference speakers who talked about working with a psychologist. It had been awhile since I had seen Dr. Hill, and I felt it was time for the girls and me to get involved. Maybe Dr. Hill could help us learn to make changes.

Jennifer and I had our first task from Dr. Hill. We were to set up rules of dialog. She didn't give us any hints other than this was about how we respect one another in conversation. We looked at each other, shrugged our shoulders and said, "Sure, we can do that."

I don't know what Jennifer was thinking, but I thought, "*I don't know how we're going to do this without some big fight.*"

Reluctantly, Jennifer and I sat down in the family room that evening. Neither of us were smiling and anyone watching us would have seen from our body language that we really didn't want to do this. It was a long and narrow room and we chose chairs that were the furthest apart.

"Are you ready?" I asked. "What should be the first rule?"

"I don't know," Jen responded. "Why are we doing this?"

I felt my stomach get restless. How could she not know? We just talked about it today.

"Jen," I said in a condescending tone. "This is what Dr. Hill asked us to do. This is so we won't fight anymore and have better conversations. Don't you . . ."

"Alright, alright, what's the first rule?"

"Well maybe it should be no interruptions. Yeah, let's start with that."

"That would be fine with me, Maybe then you'll let me finish what I have to say for a change."

"I don't interrupt you that much, and if I did I'm sure I had a good reason. Let's get on to the second rule."

Jennifer was scowling at me and I felt the tension rising in my body. I tried to control my emotions.

"You're always yelling," she said. "Maybe we should make that a rule."

That suggestion put me on the defensive. I stared at her and raised my voice.

"Well, maybe you give me reason to yell. Every time we talk you start yelling. Can't you just talk to me? Must you always have the final word? Why do you have to be right all the time? It wouldn't hurt you to listen once in awhile."

Recognizing the tone of my voice, I quickly lowered it and calmly agreed.

"No loud voices, would be helpful. What about number three?"

I paused for a moment.

"Whenever we talk, I notice that you jump to a conclusion about what I'm going to say."

"I don't do that, you do that."

"No I don't, Jennifer. You're always trying to be one step ahead of me and it doesn't work."

"What?"

She was now sitting up in the chair, using her higher pitched voice.

"Every time I try to tell you something, you interrupt and assume what I'm up to."

"Nooooo! That's what you do to me."

We continued this exchange until it dawned on us that we were both guilty of jumping to conclusions. For the first time in a while, we just looked at each other and smiled. We started to laugh at the idea that neither of us thought we were guilty yet we both saw it in the other. We now had our rules of dialogue, no interruptions, no loud voices, and no jumping to conclusions.

We worked hard at sticking to the rules, but after about a month Jennifer and I began to forget about them. We had learned from our efforts, but it was hard to maintain because we had so much emotional baggage. I think we were both afraid to let down our guard. Jennifer continued to see Dr. Hill for several months and it proved to be very helpful for her. Still my communications with the family hadn't changed. I found myself yelling and being defensive continually.

I had yet to look long and hard at me being the source for much of the family's difficulty with communications. I blamed their behavior on age, being a teen and the friends they kept. As far as I was concerned, I was making all the effort and they were not. I felt alone in this battle. If it hadn't been for the books I was reading, I would have given up.

I opened the journal I kept while reading Sari Solden's book, *Women With Attention Deficit Disorder*. I found I had listed 13 goals. I had drawn a ladder in red ink from the bottom of the page to the top. I left enough room to draw a large white cloud at the top of the ladder – sort of a landing zone. Every time I accomplished a goal, I parked the number of the goal on top of the cloud where the sun shone. Every time I failed, I wrote the number down in a circle at the foot of the ladder, or in the dump as I called it. It was a place for failed attempts. When I failed, I had to find another way to accomplish the goal.

The first goal I wrote down was creating a morning list so I could keep on task and get out the door on time. I logged my efforts.

Week of 1/13	created & posted list
	very difficult to follow
	only did it 2x this week
Week of 2/8	did it 5x this week
Week of 2/15	did it 0x this week
Week of 2/22	did it 4x this week
End of March	Yeah! list is working 6-7x a week

I tried to maintain lists every day. It wasn't perfect, but it was definitely better. Instead of never using a list, I was using it four-five times a week and that felt like success to me. I created other lists to get to bed on time, get ready to go to meetings, and lists for traveling.

Another goal was to stop my negative self-talk and get rid of the daily guilt and shame I carried. To help with this, I created an 8-piece puzzle with one negative thought or behavior on each puzzle piece.

- All or nothing thinking
- Jumping to conclusions
- No interruptions
- Negative-self talk
- Making demands or requests
- Toxic help
- Blaming and making excuses, and
- Shoulda, coulda, woulda

Before I got started, my curious mind thought that maybe my family would like to join me. So, I asked them and much to my surprise, and with some reluctance, they said, "Okay, we'll do it."

I didn't lose any time getting started.

Each week we monitored a different behavior or communication skill. I especially remember the "toxic help" week.

Toxic help was explained in different books I read "as making statements that are no help whatsoever." For example, let's say someone said they were going to stop eating fried foods to help control their weight and three months later they were caught enjoying French fries. The 'toxic' response would be, "I knew you couldn't do it. I thought you gave up fries."

Every time someone in our family was caught using toxic help, they had to restate their comment, making it positive or helpful.

This exercise was quite challenging. For four days the house was the quietest it had ever been – no one had anything nice to say!

"How pathetic. Are we that bad?"

By the third day, we were laughing because we didn't know what else to do. It took weeks to work through this puzzle piece. In the end, it had a lasting effect on us and to this day someone will lightheartedly say, "Isn't that toxic help?"

As the months went by, I worked on all thirteen goals in my journal. Not all were reached, but at the top of the ladder the cloud held more than half the goals. That was a lot of sunshine let into my life.

During my personal observations, there were several uncomfortable moments. I had discovered similarities between my behavior and that of my children.

"What's going on? I don't know if I like what I'm finding. What kind of a parent am I that didn't even know my children had ADHD, that they were depressed and anxious? Here I am doing the same things they do and not even seeing it. I'm 50 years old. How could I not see this? What have I done? I'm yelling at them for doing what I probably taught them."

I took a deep breath.

What did it all mean? Was it my fault? Do they truly have ADHD or are they just mimicking me? No, the doctors said it was ADHD and then some. No wonder they make comments like "You do the same thing, Mom." I denied it, but they were probably right.

I was in tears, thinking of the times I preached about morals and principles and how we have to be honest with ourselves.

"Here I am being a hypocrite and I'm demanding respect. Wow! This is too much. I'm beside myself. I used to think my kids hated me. Even though I knew that was ridiculous, I was beginning to wonder."

I tried to rationalize my thoughts.

"Just because they do the same things I do doesn't mean they got it from me. Look at the families Jim and I grew up in. They did this stuff all the time. Especially toxic help. So I probably learned it from them. I shouldn't be so hard on myself. And besides, the kids are big enough to know right from wrong. I can't blame myself for everything. I did my best!"

I heard myself making excuses.

"Stop!" I told myself. *"Think! Think! Clear your head and start thinking of what you are going to do next."*

My thoughts overwhelmed me.

"But what comes first? I have so much to learn about myself. I have to learn about all our disabilities, too. Then I have to teach my children. I feel like such a failure as a mom and wife."

How was I going to fix their ADHD and whatever else they had when I couldn't even handle mine? What kind of an example am I anyway? I used just as much blame and excuses as they did. Defensive? The whole damn family is defensive! If I tried to explain things to them about their disabilities and give them ways to correct their constant interruptions, they'd say, "You do it!" and they'd be right. If I tried to get them to speak calmly and more positively, they were defensive with, "Nice idea, Mom, but you're always shouting."

And they'd be right.

It took some time for me to calm down. When I did, I spent several days just taking walks and sorting through all the facts. Some days I sat and cried and prayed.

"Okay, Lord, so you've set a new challenge before me. Thanks, but I didn't ask for it. I sure hope I don't let you down."

chapter eight

One step forward

"QUIT YOUR WHINING AND DO SOMETHING!"

That's what I would say to my kids when they'd give me excuses for why they couldn't do something. Eventually I discovered it was time to take my own advice. The truth is that current knowledge of mental health wasn't a part of my life. I thought depression just meant sadness. Anxiety simply meant being overly nervous about something. And ADHD never showed up on my radar. My challenge to build a functional, loving family meant I had to understand how each of these disabilities affected everyone. Not just me.

I recalled the two coaching sessions I attended at the conference and was intrigued at the idea of becoming an ADHD Coach. But, did I need a college degree? I hoped not. Could I do this and bring in enough money to quit my job at the bank? How awesome it would be to teach people about their ADHD.

Several times Jim and I discussed my plans to become a coach. We talked about the financial obligations, setting up an office, and where my clients would come from. I got frustrated because I didn't have all the answers, but when I talked to Jim I felt my familiar enthusiastic optimism return.

"I don't know, but I just feel good about this. It'll work. Yeah, this will work. I'm sure of it."

He just sighed and said, "Okay, but I'm not comfortable with this whole thing."

I felt more strongly about this venture than anything else I had ever done. But I remembered feeling just as strongly about the failed sewing and computer businesses I had started years ago that cost several hundred dollars.

"Jim was right. How was this going to be any different?"

Yet, something much deeper told me to go for it. I didn't know what that something was, but I knew I had to do it.

I contacted several coaching organizations to find out which course would fit my needs best. I registered with the American Coaching Association and began my training. In six months I completed the course. I was eager but nervous about getting started. As my financial obligations would not be met with the coaching business at the start, I continued to work at the bank while I prepared to launch the new business. I began building a rapport with physicians in the area and established an advisory board. I designed my brochures and business cards and Jim helped me set up an office in the basement of our home. We blocked off the laundry room with curtains and room dividers. I went to garage sales and found a 1940s U.S. Navy surplus desk, a two-drawer file cabinet, a roll-around cart, and a couple of bookcases. Then I bought a round table with chairs to greet clients. It wasn't much but it was a start.

Weeks of thought went into developing programs and methods that I would need to coach. The most important one was something I struggled with daily, controlling my distractions.

"Why is it that I can't stay on task?"

I knew I consistently had a stream of thoughts in my head, but they were not necessarily related to one another. It's not like a conscious stream of thought, just random ones. Whatever I hear or see triggers another thought. As I walk from room to room, I get so distracted that I never get back to my original task. I don't do this intentionally, I just do it! When I explain it to people, they say, "Oh that happens to me sometimes."

But when I tell them it happens to me every day, all day, they have no response. Even when I'd listen to others speak, my mind would drift to other thoughts. Then I would end up changing the subject and no one would know what I was talking about.

That's when I'd hear, "You lost me."

I would also blurt out comments or jump to conclusions when someone was talking. Once I became aware of doing this, I tried to control myself, but I never made much progress.

I asked my husband, who was sitting in his favorite lounge chair in the family room, if he had as many thoughts running through his head as I had. And could he help me with my research on how to control mine.

"Sure," he said. "What do I have to do?"

"Here's a sheet of paper and a pen. I want you to write down everything you think of in the next 15 minutes. Everything! I'm going into the kitchen to set the timer and I'll do the same. When the timer goes off, we'll compare our lists."

"That's it? Just write what I think of?

"That's right. Everything!"

I went into the kitchen, set the timer and began to write down my thoughts. I wrote as fast as I could, frantically finishing up as the timer went off.

"Okay," I yelled. "Put your pen down. I'm coming in."

At first glance I was angry at what I saw since I didn't think he'd done it right.

"I did! I wrote down just what you said."

"You mean to tell me that you only thought of four things in 15 minutes!"

I wanted to shout, "Who thinks of only four things in fifteen minutes. That can't be right."

But I kept quiet.

"That's all," Jim said. "Let me see your list."

I froze. My eyes were jetting left and right. My body was tense. *Are you kidding? He wants to see my list? I can't show this to him. If he ever thought I was crazy, this would seal it.*

"No, that's okay," I said calmly. "That's all I wanted to know."

"No. This is your game and you have to show me your list."

I was panicking. I couldn't let him see that I thought of 25 things in 15 minutes. What am I going to do? How do I get out of this?

"C'mon," he said.

I smiled.

"Here. It seems like I had a lot more on my mind."

Jim looked at it and smiled, too.

"Yeah, I know. You always think like this. That's why I married you. You're always so bubbly and fun. And the kids love your creativity and all your energy. I don't know how you do it."

"What? You knew I thought like this?"

It wasn't as much fun as he thought.

"Yeah!"

I left the room scowling and frustrated, unsure of how to accept what I had just learned. I played this game with several others with similar results. My list was loaded with stuff. Theirs had fewer than ten.

So what did this mean? I needed to know.

Drawing often helps me make sense of things. I sat down and drew two blank heads representing two people who think differently. I used solid lines to create a bridge starting at that place where all information learned resides, at the base of the brain. The other end of the bridge connected to where we put our thoughts together, behind our forehead. In the first head outline, representing the non-ADHD thought process, the bridge was solid and when asked a question the person went over the bridge, found the answer, and ran straight back over the bridge to give the answer in a millisecond.

In the second head outline, representing the ADHD thought process, the bridge lines were broken in several places. When asked the same question, everything known about the answer popped into their mind, including some connected but unrelated thoughts or ideas. The broken bridge didn't allow for continuity in thought, causing this person to pause while they sorted out so many unwanted thoughts. Unfortunately, the many unrelated thoughts became distractions, causing the answer, and very often the topic, to change. (see Diagram 1).

Now I was able to see where my distractions came from.

The Bridge Story©

Who was the first president?

George Washington

uh...uh...uh...
George Washington

Not ADHD

With ADHD

What I needed to do was recognize the interrupting thought internally before it took me off on a tangent. Then, I could do something about it.

After a few weeks of practice, I was able to recognize what a distraction looked like inside my brain. For the first time I came to realize that my natural way of thinking was more about being an out-of-the-box thinker than an uninterrupted linear process. Wow! That was okay and had some huge advantages – but not when you were supposed to be focused on an important meeting topic or lecture. My mind flashed back to all those years of being misunderstood and being yelled at for not completing a chore or task. Why didn't anyone tell me this? I thought everyone thought like I did. But my problem was that I didn't know how to control my thinking. I felt so stupid. And mad! So many questions were answered by this simple bridge analogy. I began to wonder if anyone else knew this. Especially my doctors. They certainly didn't mention it. These thoughts lingered with me for weeks.

I set up an appointment with Mike Manos of the Cleveland Clinic, one of the psychologists on my advisory board, to see what he thought about this story.

I went there with some trepidation. It was still at a time in my life when I needed someone to say "You're doing okay," and trusting my instincts wasn't yet in place. Too many years of failure, negative self-talk and unwanted feedback from family and others clouded my mind. I just wanted to know if the psychologist thought my drawing and story were a good way to explain how people with ADHD think differently. That would mean a lot to me.

Once in his office, I put on my best confident look and told my Bridge story. Then I asked him my question.

"So, what do you think?"

He leaned back in his chair tapping the tips of his fingers together, looking straight at me. I waited for what seemed to be forever.

"He thinks I'm crazy! Just be calm."

Then, he sat forward.,

"What a great way to explain ADHD! This is wonderful."

Feeling relief from head to toe, I smiled and thanked him. We talked a bit longer and then I headed back, continuing to smile all the way to my office.

I couldn't wait to tell my family. We chuckled at the picture that had so many scattered thoughts in it, knowing we all related to it in one way or another. However, we still hadn't developed a way to cope with the constant flow of thoughts. We simply confirmed that it happened and didn't think much more about it.

At work the next day, I told Carol, my immediate supervisor, what I had done. She knew about my ADHD and wanted to help. She had encouraged me to find better ways to organize, and to develop strategies for getting to meetings on time. She knew I was impatient in business meetings and often caught me bouncing my leg under the table, causing the table to shake. Sometimes she sat next to me and put her hand on my knee, something that surprised me since I didn't know I was shaking the table. I was also unaware of interrupting people's sentences. I was frustrated with how complicated they could make a project instead of aiming for the bottom line. What I really wanted was to get back to my desk and do something with a little more spark in it.

I remember attending a meeting about a new project. We were discussing seven steps on the white board. I looked at those seven steps and my mind whipped through them, creating all that had to be done. I could see this as a national project, making the bank millions of dollars. I became frustrated at what I considered trivial conversation. I jumped up and went to the white board.

"See? It's real simple. All you do is . . . ."

The looks on their faces were priceless, but their comments were not.

"We don't know what you are talking about. We're on step two, not seven."

I tried to explain but it was useless. Their looks told me just how frustrated they were with my comments. Had Carol been there, she probably would have helped me out of the situation. But what really upset me about all this was that three months later at a state-of-the-state business meeting, one of the employees at that initial meeting with me, was recognized for her outstanding idea that made the project a success.

It was my idea!

Carol knew it was my idea and her hand just pressed on my knee. I guess she thought I might have something to say. I don't think anyone understands the frustrations of ADHD.

One day I was working at my desk and out of the corner of my eye I saw someone approaching my cubicle. But she was crouched down as if to sneak up on me. I just looked at her and said, "Hi."

I didn't know this person.

"Hi, I'm Mary," she whispered. "I heard you were good at helping people with ADD. Could we meet somewhere to talk? I have it, but I don't want anyone to know. I could get fired."

I was shocked. She was practically crawling up to my desk and obviously afraid of getting fired because she had ADHD. Something is wrong with that.

"Uh, sure," I said. "How about tomorrow?"

She agreed and turned around to go back to her desk. She looked back.

"Please don't tell anyone. Okay?"

"I won't say a word."

Later I learned that Carol had given her my name.

I couldn't stop thinking about her all night. She seemed to be embarrassed about having ADHD. I was not so sure I was embarrassed about that. Was I supposed to be? I felt so bad for her.

We met the next day in a quiet corner of the cafeteria and talked and laughed. Mary was afraid of losing her job because she kept making careless mistakes and was late to work nearly every day. She had been written up for not meeting job expectations and didn't know what to do. She felt very misunderstood in her professional and private life, and she hoped that I had the answers.

I told her my story about how people think differently and she loved it. Then I helped her out with a few strategies to get to work on time and a couple of ideas to help her stick to a task. I left that meeting with mixed feelings. She was so emotional and reminded me of myself as she told her story. She said she was embarrassed to have ADHD and no one, not even her doctor, seemed to be able to help her. He told her adults didn't have ADHD.

I knew her doctor was wrong.

I had educated myself quite extensively on ADHD, and with the knowledge I'd gained, I started to think seriously about becoming an ADHD Coach. But I wasn't sure if the timing was right. I realized the steady paycheck from the bank kept me there and I wasn't sure how many coaching clients I could get. So, to compensate for any loss of income, I lined up a part-time job at the community college teaching computer software programs.

Once again I toyed with the idea of going back to college.

I was personally unhappy with corporate politics and my husband was obviously tired of seeing me that way, and surely tired of my complaining.

It was time to move on.

I told Carol the next day that in a few months I would be leaving to grow my business. She was very supportive and kept her word to say nothing until I was ready. Carol was like a sister to me. She was happy with my decision and believed in what I was doing.

However, as the time to give notice drew near my insecurities flared. Could I really pull it off? I feared humiliation. What if I failed? Someone might say I told you so, or maybe just laugh at me for thinking I could do it. Was I leaving because I hated the job, or was inadequate? Could this be just another grand idea of mine that goes nowhere? The date to give notice went by. I needed one more month.

In the meantime, I read an article on people who disclosed at work that they had ADHD. It listed the pros and cons of going public. It made me curious. I knew I was leaving at the end of September, so I decided to try a little experiment and find out what happens when people divulge their ADHD secret. I discussed my experiment with Carol and she cautioned me that it might not be the smartest idea.

The first week of September, I walked by Carol's cubicle.

"I'm on my way to talk to Betsy." Betsy was Carol's boss.

Carol just smiled and chuckled.

"Are you sure?"

"What do I have to lose? I'm leaving in six weeks anyway."

Smiling, she shook her head as I walked away.

I arrived on time for my appointment and took the seat across from Betsy in her big executive chair, looking the managerial role and decked out in a suit.

"What can I do for you?"

"I need to discuss a personal issue with you."

I had her full attention.

"Recently I learned I have Attention Deficit Disorder and was told to discuss it . . ."

Two open hands flew straight up in front of my face.

"STOP! Don't say another word! I can't discuss this with you until you are registered with the bank's medical department."

With wide eyes, I sat straight up and tried to stifle a smile. I wanted to say, "I don't have the plague."

As I got up to leave, she told me Carol would know who I should contact. I calmly thanked her for her time.

Walking back to my office, I thought, *What did she think? How humiliating! You can't catch ADHD!*

While I wanted to laugh, at the same time it felt awful to have someone respond so dramatically instead of professionally.

I stopped by Carol's cubicle and we had a good laugh at the

manager's behavior. Carol gave me the number of the nurse and I made the call.

"Hello," I said. "This is Joyce and I need to talk to you about my ADHD."

The line was quiet for a moment. The nurse spoke.

"Okay, honey, what can I do for you?"

I hate being called honey!

Just take a breath, Joyce, and move on."

"I don't know what you mean. I don't need anything. I'm supposed to register my disability with you."

"Well, did you need to come in later in the morning or is this about your workload?"

"No, I don't need to come in later."

I could feel my anger growing.

"I was told to call you and register my disability."

This conversation went back and forth for about five minutes. Finally I said, "Just forget it!"

I sat at my desk feeling humiliated.

"She thought I needed to lessen my workload and get special treatment. I have more pride than that. Does everyone think that if you have ADHD you're slow?"

I was beginning to understand how a person with ADHD could become depressed or anxious.

From as early as elementary school, nearly every day I had been corrected and told how to approach things. Home life for others like me probably wasn't much better. It was always assumed I was doing something the wrong way, and before I knew it, it was happening in my family. And now, where I worked. I wondered why people couldn't understand that to do something their way confuses me. And if I had tried to do it their way, I would have failed and looked even worse.

"Why do I have to conform to how everyone else does things?"

Everywhere I worked I was corrected in procedure and told not to jump to conclusions. I was reminded not to interrupt and to keep opinions to myself. I didn't even know I was expressing an opinion. I was merely offering my advice. It seems I spent too many years being depressed over people's comments that implied I was doing something wrong or I needed fixing. I decided that disclosing was embarrassing and I would never recommend that anyone disclose their ADHD.

About two weeks later, Carol called me into her office and told me our department was being reorganized. However, I seemed to be the only one involved. I was about to become the "copy queen." Translation: I was going to spend my days copying reams of paper over and over again.

It seemed Betsy was concerned about having someone with ADHD working in the training department. If she knew anything about ADHD, she would have known that the copy queen position, with its repetitiveness, was the worst sort of job for a person with ADHD. You could walk into that copy room any time and find me wrestling with papers flying all over the place. Every time the copier didn't work, I had to re-sort the pages and make sure everything was in order. My head would spin seeing page four over there, page six stuck in the copier and page two nowhere to be found. I couldn't keep it straight in my head and in my confusion, I just threw it all out and started again. I don't think I saved them any money.

In the meantime, Carol fought hard for me to keep my original position and nearly lost her job doing so. Betsy was not about to change her mind, and didn't care to learn anything about ADHD.

The days and weeks at the copy machine bored me beyond imagination, but at the end of September, I still couldn't get up the nerve to give my two weeks notice. Even though I desperately wanted out of there, I was scared.

"Just a couple more months."

That evening my husband and I were going out to dinner for my birthday. I'd picked up the mail, pulled out my birthday cards and jumped in the car. I began crying when I read the first card, from one of my brothers.

"This is to remind you of that trusting child inside you who learned a long time ago that you have to fall a few times before you can walk. This is to help you remember the light-hearted, land-on-your-feet spirit that's within you, and, the never-give-up prizefighter you can be when you want to. This is to tell you that you've got what it takes. It's been in you all along, just waiting for you to believe again. If you ever forget, just take a look in the mirror at the wonderful, powerful person staring you right in the face – because that's the you that others see and are inspired by, and love so very much."

— Author unknown

THE NEXT DAY AT WORK I gave notice. I left in mid-October, knowing it was the right thing to do, but not knowing how it was going to work out. I walked through the last set of double doors at the bank and felt an incredible freedom. It was the last day I would stand at the copier and curse at the machine for scrunching up my originals. It was the last day I would have to listen to the corporate world dictate how my life would roll out. It was the last day I would ever take insults from people who knew less than I did about their jobs. It was the end of the flying insults, the backstabbing and insecure co-workers and all their little games they played to stay in favor with their bosses. At the same time, though, I felt compassion for many of them. Maybe they didn't have a choice of whether to leave or not. But I knew the corporate world was no place for someone like me. I was tired of it and would never miss someone telling me:

"Don't make waves!"

"Careful whose toes you step on!"

It was my turn now. I was ready to move forward, never to look back again.

There was a light at the end of the tunnel. It was not very bright at the moment, but it was there and I was ready to go for it.

With Professor Abelman, CSU 2004

chapter nine

Making the grade

AFTER THE MAIL ARRIVED, I sat at the kitchen table and flipped through Lorain County Community College's (LCCC) fall catalogue.

I sipped some tea and thought.

"Maybe I can do it this time."

That thought quickly turned.

"Oh, don't be silly. You're 50 years old and haven't read but a handful of books in 30 years. Focusing on building up my business has a better chance at success then college does. I had my chances at college and failed miserably. Why would I want to repeat that?"

A few weeks later I went to the campus library to do some research. I liked being on this beautiful campus. It's surrounded by trees and has picnic tables everywhere so students can enjoy the outdoors. I couldn't resist the urge to wander into enrollment services and ask a few questions, even though I had no intention of signing up for classes.

I spoke with a counselor who encouraged me to return to school.

"You don't have to sign up for any classes, but you might want to get the placement test out of the way. Then when you are ready to take classes, you'll have that done."

The word 'test' intimidated me and rather than talk about it, I blurted out, "Sure."

She walked me to the testing area, a fair-sized room with 15 or so tables set up and several people already working on their test. None of them appeared to be as old as me. Considering how long it had been since I'd had to take any sort of test, I was apprehensive; but I proceeded anyway. The first part wasn't too bad. The questions were on English, grammar, and reading. It was going well until I flipped the page and saw the math problems.

I froze.

My leg was bouncing up and down and my heart was racing. *"I can't do this. I'll fail this part and have to take remedial math."*

I became agitated and within ten minutes I left, throwing the test in the garbage.

"I can't believe I did that. What was I thinking?"

Walking to my car, I suddenly stopped.

"Okay, this is ridiculous. Forget the test. Just go back and talk to someone and sign up for one class. That's what you really want to do. Well, maybe two classes. I should be fine with two."

I spoke to a different counselor this time, Janet Meadows. We talked about the placement test, my past college experiences and how important a degree was to me.

In her reassuring voice, she said, "For now, let's not worry about the placement test. Let's find a class in something you like to do."

"How many classes should I take?"

"Just one."

"I'm okay with two."

She looked me straight in the eye while slowly and clearly saying, "Let's just start with one."

I just sat back in my chair.

Among the many classes, she suggested public speaking. I recalled belonging to a Toastmasters group when I worked at the bank and it seemed a natural fit. Although I couldn't explain it at the time, I felt this uncomfortable feeling of uncertainty come over me. Maybe it was just leftover fears of failure.

Mumbling, I said, "public speaking."

Straining to hear me, she said, "I'm sorry, what did you say?"

"Public speaking."

"Public speaking?"

"Yes."

The long and arduous task of applying for college and financial aid began and it wasn't long before I was registered for the Fall of '98. On the way home I stifled my excitement by reminding myself that I just might fail again, and that I needed to find a way to hide this first class from the kids. When I got home I told Jim I signed up for a class, totally expecting him to question the idea.

"Good for you. When do you start?"

"Aren't you surprised?"

"Not really. I knew someday you'd go back."

"I start in a few weeks, but you can't tell ANYONE. Not my family, my friends, and especially the kids."

A look of confusion crossed his face.

"Why not?"

"If I fail, I would never want them to know. That would just crush me. The kids already think I'm not very smart."

"What makes you say that?"

Anxiety welled up inside and I began to ramble.

"I can't even answer their homework questions, Jim. They argue with me about everything and look at me as if I don't know what I'm talking about. Don't you think that hurts? Wouldn't that make you feel bad? Stupid? I know a college degree doesn't mean you're smart, but it sure can help open doors. Besides, I want that degree. I know I can do it and I've learned a lot since the last time I took a class. All I want you to do is to keep this first class quiet. They don't have to know."

"How are you going to do that?"

"I'm taking my first class on a Saturday morning. The kids will all be asleep and right after class I'll run my usual morning errands and they won't know any different."

"Won't they see you studying?

"I'll have to try and hide that, but they'll probably think I'm just working on my women's club projects."

"Well, it sounds like you have it figured out, but I still don't understand why you don't just tell them."

"I just can't. I'd be devastated if I failed once more. So, do I have your word that you won't say anything?"

Jim nodded.

"Okay, I'll keep it quiet."

As hoped, the public speaking class was a good choice. However, every time I gave a speech I had to fight off thoughts that someone would laugh at me, or think my speech was the stupidest thing they'd ever heard. This was a different audience from Toastmasters. These were classmates and most of them were young enough to be my own child.

For our final we had to create a panel discussion. This meant brainstorming with other students. We met as a group to discuss the project, and I forced myself not to jump in with my ideas. I have a way of sounding like "You need to listen to me." Must be the mom in me.

After much discussion, someone said, "These ideas aren't going to work. Anyone have another idea?"

I can't remember what I suggested, but it was well received. I was so excited that I went out of my way and made great props and posters. I easily spent twice as much time on the project as needed. It was a great presentation and the members of the group loved my enthusiasm. It was a good feeling instead of the negative experience I thought it would be.

It was like winning the lottery when the final report card arrived. There it was . . . a big fat "A." I was pumping my fist into the air shouting.

"Yes! Yes!"

I turned up the music and sang and danced for at least an hour. When I settled down, I closed my eyes and thanked the Lord. Later that evening, smiling from ear to ear, I showed Jim the report card. He was happy for me.

"Good job! I knew you could do it."

James was home from college for the weekend. After everyone had gone to bed I posted my report card proudly on the refrigerator. The next morning as James and Kate were getting some breakfast, I stood in the hallway peeking into the kitchen. Kate spotted the report card and glanced at the grade.

"Way to go, James. You got an A."

"That's not mine."

James leaned in closer to look at it.

"Wait, that's mom's?"

He turned and saw me standing in the doorway.

"Mom, what did you do?"

"I decided to take a class at the college."

"When did you do that?"

"When all of you were sleeping on Saturday mornings."

I couldn't contain my smile.

"Why didn't you tell us?"

"I just wanted to see how I would do with one class."

"Good job, Mom. Are you going to get your degree?

"I'm thinking about it."

That's all I could say.

While everyone was excited about my going to college, James kept asking why I wouldn't tell anyone.

"No particular reason. I just did."

One evening Jim said, "I think you need to talk to James. It bothers him that you kept college a secret. Maybe you could send him an email and explain a little more."

I sighed.

"I really don't want to explain myself. I don't think I fully understand it either. It was something I had to do."

"Well, you need to say something."

I walked away shaking my head. I thought about it for a few days and decided to send James an email.

"James, the reason I never told anyone I was going back to school was because of the fear of failure in front of anyone – especially my family. What you may not know is that I have failed out of college before. So, there is this enormous amount of guilt and shame I carry. Women with ADD that are my age have gone through a life of failure [and] being shot down by the ones you love for not focusing, which adds shame to the list of emotions, and guilt for not being an achiever. I know this all sounds crazy to you, but it's a part of the ADD that is very difficult to overcome."

He seemed to be okay with my explanation. I don't know if he ever fully understood but he stopped asking questions.

The next semester I took a second class and earned a B. My confidence was building and I felt more hopeful than I'd had in a long time. With each class I was developing ways to study that helped me with recall, but tests remained difficult. It was some time before I understood that I was experiencing test anxiety. Trying to keep myself calm was difficult. I tried closing my eyes, taking deep breaths, and even putting my head down. I was simply not a good test taker and would need to start finding better ways to study. But it would be awhile before I addressed the issue of testing.

I went back to my counselor and started talking about a major in psychology. I liked the idea because it fit with the work I was doing with ADHD. The list of classes looked daunting. I realized it was time to step up the number of classes I was taking if I expected to graduate in a reasonable amount of time. In my third semester, I took two classes in my major and one less challenging class. Once again, I did well.

My first two classes taught me the importance of being organized. While organization was important to everyone, it was becoming evident that organization was essential for someone with ADHD. To survive college not only meant building strong organizational skills, it also meant building structures and strategies that fit my personal learning style. I needed a positive attitude, as well as the assistance of the college's disability services to survive the challenges ahead of me. I also needed a formal diagnosis of ADHD and any possible learning disabilities. I knew math would be a problem because I avoided it at all costs. Each semester Meadows reminded me of my math requirement should I intend to earn a degree.

"You still have your math requirement. Here's one . . ."

"I'm not taking math yet."

As I interrupted her, I sat up in the chair looking as if I were going to run out of the room.

"I'll do that last. I can't."

She just looked at me calmly.

"Why not get it out of the way so you don't have to think about it anymore?"

"No, I'm not ready. Maybe next semester. Isn't there some other class I can take that qualifies as a math requirement?"

"Yes, there is," she said. "You can take a logic class."

"Okay, let's do that."

Logic was great! I managed to get a B+, but not without help from a wonderful professor who was intrigued with my ADHD mind. Imagine that! He saw that I could solve logic problems in my head with greater ease than on paper. He sat with me one day as we worked on six logic problems. While working through the first problem, I'd interrupt him and point to another problem on the page and say, "Oh, that's just like this problem over here."

My constant interruptions caused him to cover all the other problems on the page with post-its while gently saying, "Let's just work on this one."

"Okay."

I was a little embarrassed, and smiled sheepishly.

Using a post-it to cover the other problems on the page stuck in my mind and I used it often in my studies. It then became a tool that I used in my life and in my coaching business. It fit nicely with my story on how easily distracted those with ADHD can get.

"No wonder I had such difficulty attending college in the 60s and 70s. I was paying attention to everything."

With all the difficulties I was having with learning and my seemingly unsteady emotional state, I felt it was time for an official diagnosis.

I completed a psychological evaluation in four visits. I remember how difficult it was for me to sit for the MMPI-2 test of some 560 questions. I decided to test without medication, and was quite restless. I walked around through more than half the test. At one point I was standing up, throwing my leg up on the roll-around office chair, rotating that chair back and forth just to stay alert. I was up and down and thought I was going to explode if I didn't get this testing done. They didn't need a test to tell them I was hyperactive.

Then I completed a series of tests for learning disabilities and IQ. I found some of the exercises difficult to do such as replicating a pattern with blocks. I seem to take longer to do some of the tasks than I thought I should have.

A few weeks later, I sat down with the psychologist to discuss the results. He confirmed my diagnosis of ADHD and together we went through the results. While I process information a bit slower than most, I was relieved to know that for the most part I was any average person. But to my dismay, I was average in my math abilities for my age group.

"That's not possible," I interjected quickly. "I was hoping I had a math disability so I could get out of taking math."

He smiled along with me.

"I can see that math is very intimidating for you and produces a lot of anxiety. So, I added a statement in here that says that you will need assistance and tutoring to get through math."

I felt better about that, but still couldn't see myself taking three remedial math courses and then algebra. I was certain that math would stop me from getting my degree.

He continued on to explain the various test scores and I recognized there were areas that made learning a little more challenging but certainly doable. I was very excited to see a healthy IQ for writing and a few other areas.

It was three years before I completed the math requirement. In 2001, Cleveland State University offered a summer liberal arts math class that covered algebra and geometry. This was the only class I took and Jim promised to help me, which meant he would have to do his best to ignore my inevitable melt downs and hissy-fits. What a trooper!

The first day, forty-some students showed up for class. A white-haired bearded professor with glasses walked into the room. He appeared to be in his 70s, was hunched over, dressed in a plaid shirt with khakis hanging around his hips, and stood at the front of the room staring at us. He didn't have a pencil or a piece of paper.

"Is this the liberal arts math class?" he mumbled.

We all nodded our heads and a few kids in the back of the room were saying, "Sweeeet!" I couldn't help but smile. He appeared to be too old to teach this class. I was pretty happy too because it looked as if this class would be a breeze.

Not quite! This was no traditional math course. But it was

fun and very interactive. He taught us to add, subtract, multiply, divide, and even learn algebra, using binary code. We counted daily and took our tests in binary code. I don't know about the rest of the class but everything about math was starting to click for me. And when we got to algebra, the light bulb went on. I was finally able to comprehend the concept of the missing number – the "X". That was a major achievement for me. He made math interesting and it was one of the few classes I was in where the students didn't drop out. I passed the liberal arts math class and transferred the credits back to LCCC, and my math requirements were met. Now I had every hope for completing my degree.

Statistics turned out to be the most difficult class I took. Fortunately I had been advised by Professor Emilio to make statistics my only class that semester. I took his advice and was glad I did. Three of us worked on a group project. We had gathered our data, worked really hard at understanding what we were doing, and turned it in. There was a misunderstanding in the directions on our part, and it looked like we all copied each others' work. We were accused of cheating and failed the paper. I can still remember sitting in the hallway crying.

"Me, cheat? No way!"

I was devastated.

The professor walked by and sat down to talk with me for a few minutes, listening and trying to explain what he saw. I think he believed we didn't cheat, but the grade was final. I struggled through the entire class, and from then on the professor helped me every week in his office. He was so patient while he helped me grasp the concepts. Without his guidance I would never have passed. I learned a lot, but was glad when it was over. I never wanted to see or hear about a statistic as long as I lived.

A small article appeared in the school paper about my work as an ADHD Coach and drew some attention. The next semester I was asked by the media department if I would like to be interviewed and videotaped for their Great Grads series that would play on the campus site. Because it would take place in my statistics class, I had to clear it with the professor. Once cleared, the cameras showed up in class and the interview went well.

I graduated from LCCC in 2002. My family was present, including my son and his wife, who had been married just the week before. I was worried they wouldn't be able to make the ceremony because they would be on their honeymoon. But with no prompting from me, they shortened their honeymoon to be at the graduation. I was so excited! And even more exciting was seeing my 81-year-old mom who had had open-heart surgery the year before. I had prayed daily that she would see me graduate. At the ceremony, I could see her smiling with pride. Her being there meant everything to me. Throughout those four years she encouraged me to keep going and often said, "I'm so proud of you."

The ceremony turned out to be very special. The LCCC President spoke about me in his address to the graduates. He talked about how I had persevered despite the difficult struggles and challenges of living with ADHD. He said I had dedicated myself to "receiving an education that will help herself, her family and others."

It was an emotional event as I sat there listening and recalling how people told me college wasn't for me. But I had made it. It meant so much to all of us and I couldn't help but cry from happiness.

I continued on at Cleveland State University (CSU) to earn my four-year degree. For the most part, I had understanding professors who gave me all the time I needed for testing. Still, on tests, I got D's and F's. I'd go to the tutoring center only to hear the same suggestions I had tried for so many years – read out loud, no music, take notes, highlight, focus, tape-record. All good suggestions, but something was still missing. I needed strategies that worked with my scattered ADHD thought process.

One evening my son and I talked about my new semester schedule. After reading over the syllabus, I said, "I have three tests in this class, two written papers and a term paper. That means three F's and three A's. I should pass this one just fine."

James was surprised.

"Mom? What do you mean three F's?"

"Well, I don't test well. Not because I don't know the material, but my recall is very poor. It's frustrating to think you're going to do well on a test and every time end up with a D or an F. I've just learned to accept the grade, knowing that it would never truly measure what I know. And, because I'm good at writing, I know I can pull my grade up to a C or B by acing my written papers. It's my personal formula for success."

I tried to be light-hearted and convincing so he wouldn't know how much it really bothered me to fail tests.

"Weren't you the one who told us never to give up? That we shouldn't settle for a low grade and to try harder?"

"Yes I did, but for me it's a little different. My recall is so poor because of my constant distractions that accepting it seems easier than beating my head against the wall trying to do the impossible. Maybe one day I'll figure it out. But for now I need to deal with it the best way I can."

I understood how confusing that sounded to him but it was reality.

I kept hearing how reading would open doors for me everywhere. Even before middle school I was resigned to the fact that reading was simply a waste of time for me. It was quite clear to every teacher that I was smart, but just not trying hard enough. The teachers would say something such as, "You need to focus when you read. Let's try it again."

I didn't want to disappoint them, and I wanted to believe I could do it, so I tried to focus.

"Now tell me what you read," they would ask.

"I don't know."

They looked at me as if I was trying to be difficult. I didn't know how to explain that after I would read something the words would simply fly away. Doesn't that happen to everyone? It was obvious they didn't believe me and there was no explanation for my behavior. I'd get upset and instead of crying I'd get angry and embarrassed. To hide my embarrassment, I'd make a joke and make the other kids laugh. Then, I'd just laugh back. Making something funny just felt better. Of course, then I became the class clown and that turned into a march down to the principal's office and a phone call home. It also meant that at school I got three swats with a paddle for disrespect and at home a few more. That didn't feel better.

Once in college, I was distraught that age hadn't resolved my recall problems. The slow processing of information was still evident and annoying. It didn't seem fair that others could quickly process an answer and say it. A question about slow processing was answered in *ADDitude Magazine*.

> "It means that [she] takes a bit longer than other kids [her] age to make sense of the information [she] takes in. [She] might have trouble assimilating written or spoken information, or take longer to answer questions or finish tests. This is not a matter of intelligence, as you know, but it does make it hard for [her] to demonstrate [her] knowledge."
> — *ADDitude Magazine*, retrieved 1/7/2012

This may explain why I rarely passed a pop quiz. When I started teaching ADHD students at the college level in 2011, I couldn't bring myself to give them a pop quiz. It would knowingly be setting them up for failure.

I still had to figure out how to effectively read and recall. My biggest battle was controlling the many thoughts that interfered with my focus. I'd be reading silently all the while thinking about dinner, a trip to Washington, D.C., calling a friend or analyzing what someone said to me earlier. I tried reading out loud, reading with some background noise, and having someone read to me. Through this effort, I learned that reading out loud helped me stay focused a little longer.

I also learned that dopamine is a chemical in the brain that can easily be described as a feel-good chemical. When the levels are low, you don't feel much like doing anything. With low dopamine my mind struggles to focus and therefore wanders while reading or working on a project. Not understanding this in my early years caused many books to be slammed shut. The negative messages began.

"What's wrong with me? I'm so stupid. It's only ten pages. You'd think I could handle ten simple pages. I must be going crazy."

I'd walk away and do something else, thinking that later the ability to read without distractions would just come to me.

Later never came.

The constant fear that I could fail out of college motivated me to find a solution. I knew dopamine levels in the brain rose with exercise, so I tried reading while walking on a treadmill at one mile an hour. It did help, but our furry little black dog kept trying to jump on with me and that became a distraction. If I tied him up, he'd keep barking. Now what?!

If it was distractions that kept me from focusing, then I needed to deal with that. I decided that every time I became internally distracted while reading, I would stop and write down the last sentence I remembered reading. This refocused me and I could continue to read. Because this happens several times a minute, I thought, *"This is going to take forever."*

It was very discouraging. But then I remembered how much time I wasted rereading passages multiple times and just quitting. At least this method allowed me to refocus and begin to understand what I was reading. I eventually realized that anything I wrote was far more committed to my memory than any other method I tried. Now I stood a fair chance at participating in class and tests would become much easier.

Speaking of tests, how can a person study for a test without good class notes? This was another frustration that can make a person say, "Why bother."

I would start to write down something important and just before I wrote down the last few words of the phrase, the professor would say another important phrase. I'd jump to the next line to write it down, thinking I'd remember the last few words, but no recall was available. I'd tell myself I'd get the rest of the notes from another student, but I was too embarrassed to ask. I ended up with some pretty sketchy notes with cryptic notations everywhere.

My daughter Jennifer was home from college on a weekend and offered to help me study for a test.

"Sure, that would be helpful. But I have to warn you my notes aren't the greatest."

"They're probably fine."

I was pretty excited to have Jennifer's help.

"How cool is this? Mother and daughter studying together."

She sat there looking through the notes for a few minutes and then began to scowl.

"Where are your notes?"

"Those are my notes. They're kind of a mess, but that's them."

I was a little embarrassed, feeling that someone my age ought to be able to take good notes.

"That's okay. I'll be fine."

I moved toward her and took my notebook back.

"Wait, Mom. Why don't we just talk about taking notes? Maybe that would be helpful."

My face was scrunched up by then from embarrassment and I wanted to forget it, but I didn't want to disappoint Jennifer.

"I don't know," I muttered. "I've been trying to take notes for years and I can never make heads or tails out of them. That's probably why I have such a hard time taking tests."

Jennifer was quiet for a moment.

"I can give you a few tips, if you want."

"Okay, I can use all the help I can get."

We talked for about a half hour and I came away feeling a little better after learning some tips from her such as writing down key words only, writing short phrases instead of sentences, and asking questions to clarify what I thought I heard. But something was still missing. The internal distractions were still there. I thought about how I had taught myself to park distractions on a separate sheet of paper when I was trying to do homework, and then address those thoughts later.

"Maybe I need to come up with something that will keep me focused during the lecture and forget about taking notes. But how would I remember what I had to study if I didn't take any notes?"

Then it came to me.

"I'll sit in class and listen to the lecture. Every time I catch my mind wandering, or I'm nodding off, I'll look up at the instructor and write down the next few words spoken. I can also write down key words or topics. Then when I sit down to study, I'll have a list of words and topics to look up in the text book or on the internet."

By following this system, I realized that I learned more by listening to the instructor than trying to recall what to write down. I practiced this method for one semester and saw great improvement in my grades, especially my test scores. I was now getting D's and an occasional C.

I added one more technique to studying. I started to record the class lectures, thinking I would listen to the tapes later. I was so excited about this idea that I set up an elaborate system with color-coded, mini-cassette cases for all my classes and logged the dates of the lectures on each one. In my notes, I wrote down the tape number, color and a couple key words. But I quickly learned that I kept forgetting to listen later to the tape, and it was a hassle trying to find certain parts of the lecture. I also learned that I had no patience for fiddling with the laborious system I had set up.

In talking with my colleagues about taping classes, some

said they'd forgotten to listen to the tapes, but most said they found it to be a great tool for studying. I still favored the idea of taping the classes, but how could I make it work for me? Then the light bulb came on. Since reading out loud helped me, why not listen to the tape and repeat out loud what is said? I'd be forced to listen so I could repeat word for word what was said. I could do this while driving to and from campus. That would place the content fresh in my mind for class and for tests.

It worked! I found it amazing how much more I remembered. What was even more amazing was that I could listen to a tape three and four times and still hear something I didn't hear the previous times. I guess my mind drifted and I didn't even know it. How curious.

My test scores jumped to solid C's and then one day I got a B. I stared at that B in disbelief while tears rolled down my cheeks.

The person next to me asked, "Are you okay? Did you fail?"

"No," I said. "I got a B."

He looked at me curiously. I just smiled, knowing I'd be unable to explain this one easily. I often wondered what was running through his mind.

Some professors were more difficult than others to work with. Some refused to let me take tests in the disability area. They said I could come to their office and take it. With those professors, I'd have to get the Disabilities Office involved. Most times I succeeded, but there were always those professors who obviously didn't believe in ADHD.

"Just try harder," one professor said. "I know you know the material."

"Knowing and recalling what you know are two different things."

"I'm sorry, but that is my policy."

My parting words were, "I'm sorry you just don't get it. But I need that quiet place to have even half a chance to pass the test despite the fact that I know the material."

I left very upset and felt hopeless about finishing my four-year degree.

With only four more classes to take I wanted to quit. I had made the mistake of correcting a professor during class when he started describing ADHD. He really had it all wrong and I couldn't hold my tongue any longer. I raised my hand to add my personal knowledge on the topic. I truly didn't think I was challenging him but he shut the conversation down quickly by asking me to reread the section on ADHD in 'HIS' book. Oops! He wrote the text book.

I knew I had to address the issue when he no longer called on me. He was known to be a very strict instructor but it sure seemed as if he was harder on me than ever before. I eventually stopped going to class and was issued an incomplete. I spoke with him and apologized if I offended him in class, but he didn't seem to want to acknowledge my apology. I felt stupid. We couldn't see eye to eye on how he graded my paper. There was nothing I could do to change his mind. I left his office in tears and he offered no suggestion other than to rewrite the paper by a certain date and to follow the syllabus. I was devastated. I felt this was the end of my college career.

I spent two weeks just being angry and hurt. How does a professor not want to offer help or work with you? I wanted to report him to the Disabilities Office but what was I going to say? Other than acting all pompous, he didn't do anything wrong. I owed him a paper and it had to be pretty much flawless. I did the best I could and only earned a C. I made an effort to challenge the grade, but to no avail. My 3.0 GPA was gone and I only had one semester to bring it back up.

While preparing for my final semester of classes, I realized that I was one class short of earning a degree in communications as well as one in psychology. To earn both, I would have to take a second statistics class and an additional class in communications for a total of 15 credits.

"Dare I? Could I? What about my GPA?"

I wanted to be done in one semester – not two – so I could work full time coaching people with ADHD. If I took five classes it would mean very little focus on the business. My time management skills would have to be strong, with no slacking off. I gave it a lot of thought and spoke to the communication's division head. He signed the form giving me permission to take five classes.

It was an intense year, as my business was growing. However, the challenge to keep up with both the business and college seemed to motivate me. My schedule was packed with study times and business appointments. Keeping up with classes, emails, and writing monthly articles for the local paper was an insane schedule – one I wouldn't recommend. But I persevered and successfully completed all my classes.

As graduation day neared, I filed my petition to graduate and met all the requirements. My life's dream of earning a degree was about to come true. I was excited and overwhelmed at my accomplishment. For graduation day I wanted my family to be able to pick me out in the crowd, so I used medical tape and put the word "Mom" on the top of my cap. I actually felt silly doing it, but I wanted them to find me.

Some people never march on their graduation day. I couldn't miss it. It was too important to me. A milestone had been reached.

The day arrived and I had my cap and gown all laid out. I was running around making sure everyone was going to get out the door on time. I didn't want to be late.

When I arrived I found my class and we patiently waited for our time to march. Just hearing the music brought tears of joy. What I thought was going to be a long and memorable walk seemed to go by so quickly. Then I heard my name and my heart began pounding faster as I accepted my degree. I closed my eyes for a moment and kept repeating, "I did it! I actually did it!"

In May 2004, I graduated with a double major in psychology and communications. And the best part was that my mom was there to celebrate this momentous occasion. After the ceremony, she told me, "I never doubted for a minute that you'd graduate. I am so thankful to be here."

Perhaps the most powerful personal message I received over the six years I was in college was that I was much stronger than I gave myself credit for being. I could overcome anything I needed to by changing my thoughts from *"I can't"* to *"How can I?"*

Now that I was able to work full time, I'd keep that message ever present in my mind. The college journey had come to an end and became the catalyst to an even bigger journey.

Our 24th wedding anniversary, 2001.

chapter ten

Believing

PRESSURE MOTIVATES ME. I used to think that charging through projects at the last minute made the most sense. In retrospect, it didn't work well in school, college, or my jobs. Eventually, I grew to understand what ADHD was, but I didn't know how to live with it effectively. What got in my way was my own impatience.

"Yes, Mom, patience is a virtue."

I must have said that hundreds of times. And I can still hear her response.

"When are you going to learn?"

When I first thought of starting my own business, I was concerned about my impatience. I worried about the daily battle to keep my focus on the goal. I wanted to be dependable and respected, but wasn't sure how that was going to happen.

In previous jobs, I voiced my opinion freely with what appeared to be little regard for another person's standing in the organization. Because of how fast I think, I was continually frustrated with my inability to make things move along quickly. My annual reviews reflected my frustrations. My first reviews started off with ratings of "highly efficient" in communications. But that wasn't always the case. The longer I worked in a job, the more frustrated I became with people's inability to keep up with me.

At least that's how I saw it.

My supervisor at the bank, Carol, was concerned.

"Joyce, you need to tone it down. Sometimes your frustration comes across as rude or inconsiderate."

I was hurt to hear this and really didn't see it that way.

"I'm just frustrated that people take so long to do things. I have deadlines to meet. I'd rather do things myself and then they'll get done on time. I hate waiting on people to do what seems to be so simple to do."

"All I'm saying is to tone it down."

I was reluctant to work on my tone because I didn't see myself as being rude. As hard as I tried, my "highly efficient" rating in communications took a dive to "improvement needed." Over time, I did improve my communication skills; but it felt as if I was always the one to have to make change.

As part of my improvement process, Carol asked me to participate in Toastmasters. Of course, I thought my current presentation skills were just fine. After all, I'd been training employees for five years. As it turned out, I had a lot to learn about being prepared to speak and making presentations. The critiquing by my peers in Toastmasters was invaluable – it was the first time I became aware of the impression I was giving.

My final speech was just two weeks before I left my job at the bank. In my presentation, I talked about ADHD in our family and that I was leaving the bank to help children and adults with ADHD. I felt proud that day and became emotional as I heard myself state the reality of who I am and where I was going. At my last Toastmaster meeting, I was given an engraved brass gavel. I had completed the requirements for Competent Toastmaster. Toastmasters was the catalyst I needed to move forward in my business.

I learned of the American Coaching Association during a conference in D.C. ACA teaches you to develop specialized skills in helping individuals with ADHD. I registered and spent five months going through their training. When I was done, I felt confident and much more comfortable about becoming an ADHD Coach.

After graduating from this program, I started developing my business which I called Bridge to Success Skills Training. My former supervisor helped me develop the financial side of the business, including how to charge for my services. I struggled with this part of the business for years. I had it in my head that I wasn't worthy of charging any more than $10 an hour because at that time I hadn't graduated from college.

"I hardly have much of an office and I don't even have a degree. I can't ask people to pay me more than that. I'm just starting out and I need to build more credibility to charge a higher dollar per hour."

Until I graduated from college, I continued to charge $10 an hour for my services. I worked hard to build my reputation. I found that being an ADHD Coach was extremely rare in Ohio. It was my job to make my presence known, as well as what I could do for those with ADHD. I contacted my local high school and got permission to do my first presentation. It drew about 50 parents and students.

Using visuals, I started to tell the Bridge story of how people think differently. A young boy about the age of ten with red hair and lots of freckles left his mom's side and worked his way up to the front row. He sat cross-legged about 20 feet in front of the screen, never taking his eyes off of me. I looked at him and smiled. He smiled back. When I showed the picture of how scattered some people think, he had tears rolling down his cheeks. My heart took a dive.

"What did I say? Where is his mom?"

I kept speaking and every time I looked at him he was wiping away another tear. When the presentation was over, he got up and ran back to his parents.

A number of people lined up to ask questions and I kept thinking, *"That poor little boy. What did I say to upset him?"*

After answering people's questions, I looked up and there in the back of the room was the little redhead with his parents. I walked over to him.

"Hi. What's your name?"

"Patrick."

"Did you like the story I told, Patrick?"

He spoke excitedly.

"I tried to tell my mom that I'm too confused to do my homework and she wouldn't believe me. She thinks I'm lying."

"Is that why you were crying?"

"Yes," he said softly.

His mom and dad stood there, obviously surprised at what he had to say.

"Well, maybe Mom didn't know about this story."

"But I told her. I told Dad, too."

I could hear the frustration in his high-pitched voice. His eyes were filled with tears. I related to him more than he knew.

I knelt down.

"Sometimes parents don't understand. Maybe today's story helped your mom and dad to know what you mean by being confused. How about if I talk to Mom for a minute while you stay here with your dad?"

Patrick's mom said she'd never seen him so emotional or talkative about anything.

"Patrick kept saying, 'I told you, I told you.' My husband and I learned a lot from your story. I don't think we realized just how different his thinking was but now we do. This was an eye-opening experience for us, too."

We spoke a little longer and I assured her that Patrick's way of thinking was normal for him. Unfortunately, the many distractions in his mind as well as the ones all around him made it difficult for him to finish homework or focus in class. I suggested she take my workshop for families to help Patrick learn about taking ownership of his ADHD.

I hadn't developed the workshop yet, but I knew in the back of my mind that I could do this. Others would see this as shooting from the hip. Maybe they'd be right.

Within a month, I'd developed the workshop with the Bridge story being the foundation of the course. The first three sessions would be with the students. Sessions four and five were for parents and the sixth session was with the whole family. Now, I was ready to start my first workshop.

Nine families with hyperactive boys between the ages of 9 and 12, including Patrick, registered for the class. I thought, *"C'mon Lord, could you make the first one any tougher?"*

As each parent dropped off their child, they asked if I needed any assistance. I would just smile and say, "Thank you but they won't be any trouble."

"Oh, you don't know my son," said one mom. "I'll be right outside the door if he gets out of hand."

"Okay, but don't worry."

Well, I was a little worried, but I was also confident I could manage them. The boys looked at me with their toothless smiles, legs swinging away beneath the chairs, and pencils tapping on the table. Their bodies were turning around and looking at everything possible and their eyes could hardly stay still. Every sound they heard made them turn and look. As I called their names, they would turn back to me.

I handed out a blank outline of a head. The plan was to have them draw on it as I told the story about distractions. Before I got to the first instruction, all of them had drawn eyes, ears, a nose, a mustache, and a lot of spiked hair.

"Hmmm," I thought. "That didn't go so well. What's plan B?"

I handed out another head outline instructing them to wait until I told them what to draw. That went much better and I got through the story.

For the next part I decided to engage them using questions and answers. However, when I asked a question they didn't just raise their hand, they shot it into the air. Some just blurted out their answers and started telling very long stories. They were now laughing and having a great time talking to one another.

"Hmm. What's plan C?"

To manage the interruptions, I let them help me develop a signal that meant their story was too long. One of them suggested I just say "shut up already."

Quickly, we agreed that didn't sound very nice.

What we did agree on was for me to hold my finger up and spin it in a circle. That worked quite well. The kids were much more attentive and learning began.

Throughout the first three sessions I planned different ways to keep them focused on their work. By being a team we became good at spotting distractions, not blurting out our answers, and writing down those extra thoughts that were not about our discussion.

When the student sessions were over, the parents came together for the next two sessions. They learned how best to support their child, create simple strategies, and give their child the confidence to own their ADHD behaviors. They were brimming with questions.

What upset these parents the most was that people saw their child as a troublemaker or willful. Their child was labeled uncooperative, interruptive, impulsive, or a daydreamer. Parents were tired of being told they needed to discipline more. It concerned me, too, but I reminded them that our time is better spent teaching our children to believe in themselves and improve their self-esteem than to be concerned about what others thought. I was there to help these families develop ways to cope with ADHD and keep the family unit solid.

The final week, both parents and children attended. This was the week when barriers within the family began to break down. Everyone understood that the goal was to work as a team to make the child a more productive student and a happy family member.

I was unsure of my impact on each family every step of the way. I waited for someone to tell me I didn't know what I was doing. Instead, they were amazed at how well I related to them and the children. I was pleased and excited for these families.

By word of mouth, the first family workshop attracted other families. And I was learning from them as much as they were learning from me. The stories of how children were treated and misunderstood were heartbreaking. Over the years it became apparent to me that schools and physicians had much to learn beyond the diagnosis.

One of the things I did to build credibility was to develop a professional advisory board that consisted of therapists, a neurologist, and an M.D. We met several times to discuss the direction of the business and the programs I offered. It was very beneficial. My first adult ADHD client, who was quite a challenge, was referred to me by one of my advisory board members.

Susan had ADHD, anxiety, obsessive-compulsive disorder (OCD), and oppositional defiant disorder (ODD). My primary objective was to focus on helping this 26-year-old, divorced mom, with a two-year old daughter and several cats, become more organized and a better manager of time. When she came to me, she was using six time-management techniques, all at the same time. Her first tool was a calendar with a month overview on her kitchen cupboard. That system was supported by sticky notes on the pantry door, a two-month planner in her purse, a daily review sheet posted on the back door, a fancy daily planner, and 3x5 index cards to break down her many projects and goals.

"Oh my gosh! I'm being put to the test. Why couldn't the first one be less complex?"

But I wasn't about to turn down my first client.

The year I spent coaching Susan was filled with many challenges. She felt secure with all her systems, and just wanted to coordinate them and become more functional. I was overwhelmed looking at all the systems and didn't know how organization was going to happen. But Susan was determined to improve and worked hard on the strategies introduced.

Our mutual goal was to make her daily planner the main source for managing her time. To do that, it was important that all her sticky notes come off the cupboard doors and be entered into her planner. Having anxiety and OCD made it difficult for Susan to throw them away, so for several weeks she stored the sticky notes on the day she was to do a particular task even though it was already entered in her planner. Eventually, when she felt comfortable, she threw them away. After several sessions she began trusting herself enough to throw away her sticky notes immediately after she entered them.

Another barrier was Susan's inability to stay on task and complete a project by the deadline. Her occupation was translating manuals from English to Spanish. That seemed straightforward, but Susan often had ideas about making the document more precise by changing the format or adding additional sections. Her ideas may have been great but that wasn't what the company wanted from her. As a result she had to ask for extensions. This was time that could have been used for new contracts that would generate more money for her. Together, we came up with a plan – add an addendum to the final translated document, suggesting her ideas. That way, she could meet her deadline and be considered for more paid work.

It was a year of persistent effort and compromise that resulted in her eliminating all but two of her time management methods. I'm certain I learned as much as she did.

My ability to help those with ADHD was growing stronger. I began presenting to families throughout Ohio. Also, I was teaching ADHD undergraduate students at Cuyahoga Community College in Cleveland how to manage ADHD in college, as well as teaching graduate students at Notre Dame College.

Marketing my business was, and still is, my least favorite job. Not because I couldn't do it, but because it was time consuming and I had a lot on my plate – a growing business, a senior in high school, two kids in college, going to college myself, a home to keep up, and spending time with my dear husband.

I had started working one-on-one with adults with ADHD, another new experience. I learned quickly that many of their challenges were the result of a lack of time management. I knew from my own experience just how crucial planning was to managing my ADHD. Now I had to figure out how to help others believe that managing their time does work. I had bought several different types of planners but found keeping up with them on a daily basis overwhelming. I would last two or three days – maybe a week if I were lucky – then I'd either forget about using it or simply lose it. Planners were my nemesis.

As I coached, it became apparent that clients continually overbooked themselves. I recognized their need to see where their time went each day. Each time I coached, I started drawing lines on sheets of paper and wrote times down the left side. I asked clients to plan their goals for the day, including time to go through their morning routine, work, driving, eating, relaxing, and a multitude of other required tasks. As they returned each week, I listened to their frustration of not having enough time in a day to finish what they envisioned as possible to complete. Seeing their projects and tasks on paper was a reality check on how many hours are actually in a day. It was having a great impact on the adults.

By 2002, my informal planning system of stapled sheets of paper, started looking like a real planner. I challenged myself to develop a planner specifically for coaching. It would become a workbook that all my adult clients had to learn to use as part of their coaching experience. I referred to it as a planning journal instead of a time-management system. Planning for those with ADHD was not just managing time, there was much more depth to it than that.

My planner did not have pictures, three monthly calendars at the top of the page, or anything to distract them from the task of planning. But most importantly, the planner had a full page of 15-minute increments of time from 7 AM to 12 midnight. With ADHD, the visual of seeing where time goes is not just a good idea, it's essential. The planner also contained a block on every day to jot down distractions. Later, those distractions could be planned and placed on the appropriate time lines.

Our youngest daughter Kate had started her first year at The Ohio State University (OSU) around the same time I was developing the college planner. It hadn't been tested yet. I didn't realize how much she needed planning skills until it became evident from the numerous late night calls. Kate seemed to be anxious and overwhelmed. She didn't feel well.

In her frantic state, I couldn't get her to go to the hospital. Not until I used my "mom" voice did she call her sister, who was also at OSU, to take her to the hospital. I left at 1:00 a.m. and drove two and a half hours to meet her at the local hospital. By the time I got there she was released and diagnosed with mono, strep, and dehydration. I stayed the night with her in the dorm. I didn't get much sleep as I was so worried about her. The next day I brought her home for a couple weeks. She began to talk about quitting.

"Quitting?" I said. "Not a chance! What's going on?"

She started to ramble.

"I'm too far behind in everything and I'll never catch up. This is crazy. I can't do this. I'm dropping out now."

I placed my hands on my forehead and thought.

"Think, Joyce, think. Your daughter wants to quit."

"Why are you behind in your studies?"

"It's just too much."

"Kate, what are you doing with your time during the day when you are supposed to be studying?"

Very nonchalantly she said, "Playing Frisbee on the oval."

The oval is a large grassy area at the center of campus.

I shook my head.

"I don't understand."

"We play Frisbee on the oval every day."

She was becoming indignant.

I just closed my eyes for a moment to gain composure.

"All right, but when do you do homework?"

"On Sunday night."

"Sunday night? This isn't high school, Kate. Maybe that's why you're behind in your studies. I can't imagine trying to get all your reading and homework done in one evening. Are you using your OSU planner?"

She just looked at me with nothing more to say.

"Kate, I just finished developing the college planner and I haven't tested it yet. Let's get your books and see if we can work this out."

"I'm not using your planner."

She stood there with her arms crossed, eyes glaring, and lips curled down.

"Kate, let's just try it. I want to know if it'll work. That's all."

I realized I was pleading.

"I'm not using your stupid planner."

With the low, calm-but-firm voice moms use when they mean 'do it or else' I said, "Go get your books."

Kate stomped up the stairs and returned with books, dropping them on the table.

Now I was being tested. Could I really get more than 400 pages of reading and makeup assignments planned into the new planner? It was only two weeks before she had to return.

With confidence and a little attitude, I forged ahead.

"Sit down and let's get started. When we're done, you can take the planner and throw it in the fireplace. I don't care. I just want to see if it will work."

She refused to sit down, and informed me that she was going to a baseball game with her brother that weekend.

"You aren't going anywhere, honey. You have strep, mono and you're too far behind in your work."

But the attitude in her voice told me not to challenge her. I simply ignored her comment and continued working.

When I was done, all her assignments were entered into her planner, as well as time to sleep and recover. She took the planner and just said, "Hmm." But she followed the plan and eventually caught up with her work in time to return to campus with a new outlook and a new planner.

From that experience, the final planner, Plan for Success: College©, was published. Kate went on to use the college planner and stayed in college.

The first place I used my adult planners was in the six-week workshops I developed for adults with ADHD. It was held six times a year. All my adult clients must go through six weeks of education on what it means to be ADHD and how it affects them cognitively, emotionally, and behaviorally. It is a course of self-observations, developing skills, and learning time management the ADHD way. Without this education, their emotional state of mind would get in the way of achieving their goals during one-on-one sessions.

Over the years, I had gained the respect of my clients. Gaining that same respect from therapists, physicians, or even educators was more challenging. That took several years.

While my advisory board understood that I was educating and teaching life skills, other professionals were not sure what I was doing. Therapists felt I was providing therapy without a license. Educators who claimed to be coaching ADHD people using the title of tutor, learning specialist, or counselor believed they didn't need an ADHD Coach. Other professionals felt that if they had ADHD themselves, that it further qualified them to help those with ADHD.

Having grown up with ADHD I knew it wasn't that simple.

From elementary school on many people tried to help me, but to no avail.

Teachers kept giving me good advice, but because I had ADHD I was unable to follow that advice consistently. No one seemed to understand that I did know what to do. I just couldn't make it happen. It wasn't intentional. My mind continually wanted to explore and I couldn't hold a thought for longer than ten seconds. What I needed was to first understand how my brain worked, and what a distraction felt like so I could identify the thought as a distraction and stop it.

As I got older, doctors and therapists couldn't help me. It was frustrating and depressing to hear people tell me over and over again that I needed to "just stay focused" or "tackle one thing at a time" or "You're not trying hard enough."

Once a doctor told me to read an article and we'd talk about it on my next visit. I took the article thinking, *"Is he crazy? Doesn't he know that most people with ADHD can't remember what they read? And, even if they did read it, they wouldn't be able to discuss it with anyone that day, let alone next month."*

I knew the doctor meant well, but he just didn't get it.

On the other hand, I can't imagine how frustrating it was for a therapist to give me a pep talk, or a skill or strategy only to hear me say "I already tried that," or "It won't work anyway." What is a doctor supposed to do if the patient shoots down every effort without giving it a try? I had assumed that therapists knew more about ADHD than I did and that they would have some concrete answers that would make this frustrating life go away.

OVER TIME PHYSICIANS AND THERAPISTS began to understand that ADHD Coaching was not about therapy but about managing life skills. As a coach it was my job to recognize depression and anxiety and get the student help from the appropriate place. ADHD Coaching often lifted depression and anxiety, but for many, therapy was needed as a collaborative intervention.

Slowly, through client referrals, physicians became curious and started asking questions.

"Hi, is this Joyce Kubik?"

"Yes it is. How can I help you?"

With great enthusiasm in his voice, Dr. Giavani said, "I'm a family practitioner and I would love to know just what you do. A week doesn't go by that your name doesn't come up."

I smiled.

We spoke awhile and I explained my coaching model for adults with ADHD. About six months later, Dr. Giavani signed up for my adult ADHD workshop. It seemed his wife had heard of me and thought he needed the help. Dr. Giavani became a great advocate of my work, referring adult patients to me nearly every week. Over the next several years, I found myself speaking at physician's offices, and hospital grand rounds.

As the business progressed, I set my sights on being published. My first two articles appeared in a national publication called *ADDitude Magazine*. I was dancing around the house filled with excitement. Jim and the kids were proud of me and that's all I needed to know. But if anyone outside my family said anything that sounded like praise, I'd change the conversation and move on.

While I knew in my heart that I was doing well, I still feared failure. There seemed to be this constant reminder that failure was still an option. It was like a gray cloud following me everywhere. I wished it would leave.

It wasn't until I'd earned two college degrees that I felt worthy to be called successful. Soon after, I was asked to deliver the keynote address for Disability Awareness Day at Cuyahoga Community College in Cleveland. Wow! Me, a keynote speaker? I could hardly believe it.

The room was filled with students and influential people in the community. My mom came with me and we were guests of honor at the president's table. Guests of honor! Imagine that! Then it was time for me to speak.

I felt fine until my introduction began. My heart was racing and I thought I was going to faint. I took quiet, deep breaths as I walked up to the stage. I began to speak. Out of the corner of my eye, I saw someone moving their arms all over the place. It was distracting and annoying. I hoped someone would see this person and ask them to sit down. After all, I was giving the keynote.

But no one did.

At the risk of losing focus, I glanced toward that person and to my surprise she was signing my speech. My ADHD mind became so distracted that I began looking for the hearing impaired reading her sign language. I stammered a bit in my speech, but fortunately, I regained focus quickly. It was a successful day.

I began looking for organizations that were about ADHD Coaching and came upon the ADHD Coaches Organization (ACO). It was a young organization and on the move. I quickly learned that ADHD Coaches from around the world look to this organization for guidance. Since I love being an active part of anything I belong to, it wasn't long before I was on the board as Program Chair and then Conference Chair. It was, and still is, an exciting organization with which to work.

It was clear my life had taken a new direction and it was time to resign from the Women's Club of Avon Lake/GFWC in Ohio that I had belonged to for twenty years. But not before writing a resolution for Mental Health Parity with other clubwomen. This resolution was about the discriminatory insurance coverage of mental illnesses, as well as the stigma placed on mental illness. Its resolve was that member clubs of the General Federation of Women's Clubs (GFWC) were urged "to promote programs that educate members and the public about the connection between mental and physical health in an effort to remove the stigma associated with mental illness

. . . That the General Federation of Women's Clubs supports legislation and regulations requiring equitable coverage for mental and physical illnesses."

The Ohio Federation of Women's Clubs/GFWC, gave me the opportunity to grow and the courage to make changes. Leaving the organization was a difficult decision to make, but one that was necessary.

Throughout my journey I have always kept a positive and forward-thinking attitude. The Law of Attraction states:

> "The action of Mind plants that nucleus which, if allowed to grow undisturbed, will eventually attract to itself all the conditions necessary for its manifestation in outward visible form."

In other words, you have the ability to will your direction. It was time to take inventory of all that I was doing.

I'd learned a lot over the years and it was time to reassess my direction and the management of my business. After all, I'm still ADHD and have some of the same problems my clients have.

Graduation Day CSU, 2004.

chapter eleven

Rules

A BUSINESS PLAN PROVIDES a company the focus it needs to reach a specific goal. To reach that goal, you must stay on task and keep up with the organizational needs. Those needs include good communication skills, meeting deadlines, and maintaining your integrity by being prompt, honest and courteous.

My two previous efforts to start a business failed because I had no strategies in place to control my ADHD outcomes. I simply got up each day and did what had to be done. I worked long hours and made very little money.

This time it would be different.

The first few years I was coaching, I struggled to stay focused. Every day was overwhelming and all I did to maintain the business was to push myself to meet the daily deadlines. Everything was a crisis. With the knowledge of how my ADHD affects every aspect of my life, I came to realize I needed to coach myself as I did my clients.

The planner had to become the most essential tool. I made a rule that anything that came across my desk or into my mind had to be written into the planner and planned on the time lines. Time lines ran from 7:00 a.m. to 12:00 a.m. It was my only way to control my inattentive and impulsive lifestyle that I'd had for so many years.

That rule worked very well for me, and many more were to follow. Most of them evolved over my years of personal observations and coaching my clients.

"Write everything down," I'd say to my client.

"Let's lay out a plan to get all your assignments done. Then all you have to do is follow the plan. You can check in with me each day and let me know your progress. A check-in is a simple phone call to my office stating you have completed your tasks for the day, or moved them to another day."

"How am I going to remember to check in? I'm always day-dreaming or off on some tangent," he'd say.

"Well, let's make a rule. Write 'check-in' on a colorful piece of paper and place it where you can see it in the evening to remind yourself to look at your planner, plan your next day and then do the check-in."

"That's a good idea. I think that will work."

It was a good idea, but not the complete answer. Clients kept forgetting to check in. During the coaching session, they would express how bad they felt because they couldn't remember to do a simple check-in. They'd thought about the check-in but the thought left their mind within seconds.

I decided to examine my own use of a planner, as well as checking in with myself. And, yes, I found it challenging to do every night. I eventually came to the conclusion that a rule alone wouldn't make me stay on task. I needed to train myself to become more disciplined about following rules.

Forgetting was an everyday thing for me. If it weren't for the negative outcomes of forgetting, I'd have to believe it was a norm for me. I'd get started working on a project and without realizing it, I'd drift off to another project that caught my attention. An hour later I realized I hadn't finished the first project. Getting myself to return to the first project, which had a deadline, was nearly impossible.

Forcing myself to avoid acting on distractions was a challenge. I started by monitoring internal distractions that took me away from my current project. On a good day, I'd write down the distraction and attend to it later. Too often, I'd simply rationalize with myself that the distraction was more important. I would get to the original project shortly. I knew it wouldn't happen – I had little discipline. Then, as usual, at the end of the day I was beating myself up for not doing the one thing that had to get done.

Discipline meant forcing myself to do something I didn't want to do. At times I felt I was disciplining a child – me! I'd even have my very own little hissy-fit! Then I would do what I had to do. I actually found a mug that said, "Don't underestimate the power of a hissy-fit." It's right where I can see it everyday to remind me that rules are made to be followed and you can scream and yell all you want, but do what you gotta do.

Rule 1. Discipline yourself to stay on task.

Rule 2. Check your planner 2 to 3 times a day.

Checking your planner 2-3 times a day is not that easy when your mind is distracted every ten seconds. Very often I would hyperfocus on a project and completely miss an appointment, or the fact that I was supposed to stop and work on another project.

I learned to set timers on my phone to remind me to check my schedule. I also put a note on my table, where I relax in the evening, as a reminder to check and plan my next day.

Rule 3. The planner has a home – use it.

"Where's my planner? I just had it! Who knows where my planner is?"
There is nothing more frustrating than the hunt to find your planner – or most anything else for that matter.

I had to find a home for my planner: the counter, the bench, the corner of my desk or in my book bag. It just made life so much easier.

Rule 4. Delegate.

"Delegate? Why would I want to do that?"
By the time I explain the task to someone I could have it done. And it would be done the way I wanted it done. After much thought, I came to the conclusion that I was afraid to delegate. Not because I didn't want help, but what if I gave someone the wrong information? I might get yelled at for forgetting one of the steps. Then I'd feel like a failure once again.

But I had to be honest. There are only 24 hours in a day and I need to sleep. I had to challenge myself to slow down when I explained directions. I needed to hear what I was saying. Hearing seemed to aid my recall. I also made sure that after I'd explained the directions I said something to the effect of, "I hope I didn't miss anything. Just ask questions if something doesn't seem right." It took a while to be comfortable about delegating, but it has saved me a lot of time.

Rule 5. Never email before breakfast.

For me, emailing before breakfast was a great weight loss program. But not a good health choice. Mornings were filled with a constant flow of thoughts. I'd write them down so I wouldn't forget. Then, I'd run down to my office, which is in my basement, and start doing everything on the list.

I'd get so wrapped up in answering emails, and working on projects, I wouldn't get to breakfast until somewhere around 2:00 or 3:00, even though I was starving. Eventually I learned to discipline myself not to open the basement door until I had eaten my breakfast.

Rule 6. Lists are your friends.

Before using lists to manage my ADHD, I used lists to make sure my kids knew what it meant to clean the bathroom or any other room in the house. Every week it was the same battle.

"Yes, that means cleaning the mirror, and emptying the garbage."

I got tired of repeating myself every week about their responsibilities. So I created how-to lists and posted them discreetly in each room.

I recalled this strategy as I recognized my own forgetfulness with daily routines. I now have lists for morning and evening routines, business procedures, event planning procedures and more. Lists are lifesavers.

Rule 7. Be prepared for all meetings.

"See you in ten minutes," said my colleague.

"What's in ten minutes?"

"Staff meeting."

"Oh, yes. I knew that!"

Now it's scramble time.

"Shoot, I didn't do . . ."

Then I'd either have to work furiously to gather my stuff together for the meeting, or I'd have to start fabricating my best excuse.

Now I own my own business and I'm accountable to myself. I had to find a way. As meetings were scheduled, I made myself put it in my planner. I took it one step further and planned time to be ready for the meeting. What a great feeling it was to be prepared. I didn't have the stress of coming up with yet another excuse for not being a team player.

Rule 8. Don't call yourself out.

I'd walk into a meeting a few minutes late. Then I began.
"Sorry I'm late again," or
"You wouldn't believe why I'm late."
In my personal life it wasn't any different. I kept explaining to everyone why I was late or forgot to bring something.

By doing this I let everyone know of my shortcomings. I made it clear to them that I was forgetful, full of excuses, and unreliable.

I began to watch people's reactions to other people who arrived late for meetings. I noticed this one person who always came in late and never said a word. He just sat down and started participating. No one gave it a second thought – at least out loud.

"Huh," I thought. "No one ever questions him or makes comments to him like 'Don't worry, we expected you to be late,' and then laughs. I decided that's how I wanted people to treat me."

The next meeting I did what he did – I kept quiet when I entered the room. I didn't draw attention to myself. People still saw that I was late, but after several times of acting like this, I was no longer hearing negative comments.

I also paid close attention to how often I called myself out for things that didn't go well at home. I worked hard – and still do – to manage the way in which others perceive me.

Rule 9. Don't interrupt.

There's a simple reason why I interrupt. I instinctively know I will forget if I don't immediately say what I'm thinking.

After all, my brain has been with me a very long time. It knows I'm going to forget and pretty much nags at me to 'just say it.'

That made perfect sense to me.

However, the problem of interrupting still remained. I taught myself to write down in just two or three words what I wanted to say. When the right moment came, I had a reminder right in front of me. But we don't always have the opportunity to write something down. Sometimes, it's just not appropriate.

I taught myself to say, "Excuse me, don't let me forget to tell you . . ." or "Let me jot a quick note down so I don't forget something I need to tell you."

It's a polite and simple way to save those thoughts and not interrupt.

Rule 10. Take comments at face value.

Before I understood my ADHD, I thought everyone was accusing me of doing things wrong. They only had to say, "I can't find . . ." and I immediately came back with, "I didn't have it last. What makes you think I did anything with it?"

Then the argument would start because they felt attacked.

I taught myself to listen and not let my mind create something that wasn't there. Whatever the statement or question was, I needed to let go of the battle within me to defend myself. I needed to simply answer the question. I had to believe that if they meant something more by their statement or question, they would let me know.

I found it nerve-wracking at first, but eventually got used to it.

Rule 11. Avoid long explanations.

I noticed that I couldn't just answer a question without going into some long explanation that appeared to bore the listener.

For example, "Did you remember to drop the mail off at the post office?"

Of course I'd forgotten and the long explanation began.

"Oh, crap, I wanted to but I was already late and got caught up in traffic. You can't believe how crazy people drive and they don't have any common sense. I was so upset about work and the drive home that I completely forgot. I remembered, I just got all upset. Will tomorrow be okay?"

For starters I had to accept the fact that I am guaranteed to forget. There is a lot of time between the morning when I am asked to do a task until the time I head home from work. To ask myself to remember was setting myself up for failure.

I started by putting the task on a post-it note and taping it to the center of my steering wheel or on the dashboard. There was still the possibility I would not see the note, but that rarely happened. Writing the task in my planner was helpful but by the time I got to the car, I'd already forgotten. Using a visible cue as a reminder worked best for me.

Rule 12. Think before you speak.

My mom said, "Count to ten." It was supposed to keep me from saying something foolish or incriminating. Counting to ten didn't work.

What did work was to ask myself two things before I spoke.

What is the purpose of what you are about to say? And, what can you expect?

This allowed me to filter and decide if what I was about to say would produce a positive outcome or at least the outcome I wanted.

Rule 13. Advocate for myself.

Too often I sat back and let people direct my life. I let sales people tell me what I needed. I didn't speak up and say, "I don't need that" or "I don't have time."

If I had strong feelings on a particular topic, I was easily swayed because I didn't want anyone to get upset if my opinion was different. I wouldn't say no to questions that deserved a no. I wanted to please everyone.

I was upset with myself for not standing up for my beliefs. Making changes in this area meant going through some therapy where I learned how to believe in myself. I had to look at my accomplishments and recognize my strengths. With the therapist's help, I became good at believing in myself so I could advocate for myself.

Rule 14. Stop the negative self-talk.

What really surprised me was how good I was at beating myself up with negative self-talk. If there was an award for this self-inflicted pain, surely I would win it.

Through journaling, I began to see the negative impact it had on my life. I paid a heavy price for the buildup of those negative messages – loss of self-esteem, failing out of college twice, and poor job performances.

I taught myself to turn a negative thought into a positive one. At first it was 20 and 30 times a day, but over time it became less frequent. I could live with that. Not using negative self-talk greatly changed my attitude and outlook on life.

Rule 15. Get control of your anxiety.

My ADHD brought many anxious moments in my life. To gain control, I learned how anxiety happens in the brain. Then I monitored those thoughts that escalated my anxiety. They were words and phrases that told me I couldn't do something, I'd never succeed, I was stupid, and I was lazy. These phrases were my first cue. Once recognized, I could stop the self-defeating language and calm myself.

Most importantly, I had to teach myself to think in terms of how can I, instead of I can't. Every time I found a barrier in my life, I analyzed it and built a successful strategy around it.

AS A RESULT OF FOLLOWING THESE RULES, life has become an unforgettable journey. I have achieved goals that I never would have thought possible. I'm not afraid to try and 'can't' is not an option. Not only am I engaged in my business, but I'm engaged with life all around me. I don't hate having ADHD, I'm excited about it.

I encourage you to create your rules by observing your behavioral outcomes and then developing strategies and structures that will build positive life changes all around you. It doesn't matter if you choose to do it on your own, or accept the help of a therapist or ADHD Coach. It only matters that you do it!

With Dr. Roy Church, President LCCC, 2004.

Rules for Getting Along with Your ADHD
Joyce Kubik, CMC

Rule 1.   Discipline yourself to stay on task.

Rule 2.   Check your planner 2 to 3 times a day.

Rule 3.   The planner has a home – use it.

Rule 4.   Delegate.

Rule 5.   Never email before breakfast.

Rule 6.   Lists are your friends.

Rule 7.   Be prepared for all meetings.

Rule 8.   Don't call yourself out.

Rule 9.   Don't interrupt.

Rule 10.   Take comments at face value.

Rule 11.   Avoid long explanations.

Rule 12.   Think before you speak.

Rule 13.   Advocate for yourself.

Rule 14.   Stop the negative self-talk.

Rule 15.   Get control of your anxiety.

Preparing for Grand Rounds, The Cleveland Clinic Foundation, 2008.

chapter twelve

Greater outcomes

IT GOES AGAINST MY NATURE to follow rules. I'd rather go with the flow. But I proved over and over that going with the flow didn't work – structures and strategies did. Seeing the positive results of careful and thoughtful planning made it easy to mentally invest in my future. Knowing that, I enjoyed setting one major goal every year. I never quite knew how I was going to achieve it, but I was confident the law of attraction would get me there. That and following my rules.

After a few years of working with students and adults, I felt a need to explain to people what living with ADHD was really like. I was troubled by how much ADHD was misunderstood. One of my first goals was to write for the local newspaper, *The Press*.

I contacted the *The Press* and pitched the idea of a monthly article on ADHD. My first article "Jonathan asks: why am I so hard to understand?" appeared in 1999. I was so thrilled to see my first byline that I sent a copy of my article to everyone in my family as well as friends and associates. I continued to write monthly articles for about three years. As time went by, I learned that readers were sending my articles to family members and friends across the country. It was good to know that what I had to say pleased my readers.

When I felt established as a writer, I ventured into writing for a national publication, *ADDitude Magazine*. "Park Your Thoughts at the Door" was published in 2003. In it, my first mantra appeared "Just because you think of it, doesn't mean you have to do it." The concept was to allow myself to put aside thoughts that did not pertain to the task at hand. A second article appeared in *ADDitude Magazine*, in 2008. This was an interview with a 59-year-old client, Claire, and her experience in working with a coach. She had taken my six-week workshop through conference calls. Her story told about her success in learning to manage her ADHD world, and implementing techniques learned in the workshop.

My confidence grew every year and it was time to expand beyond the local area.

"The Successful ADHD Student" was a popular two-hour presentation for families that I'd been doing for several years. Since I'd never been trained in developing workshops, I simply used the skills I learned from my training classes at the bank. Wanting to have a greater impact, meaning a more skills-based program, I took that two-hour presentation and developed a two-day workshop that involved both the parents and the children. For two days, eight to ten families worked together with their child to build a strong understanding of the affects ADHD has had on their child's life, as well as on the family unit.

In this workshop I intentionally had parents go through three questionnaires with children other than their own. This was important because parents came to the workshop frustrated with their *own* child. Many parents found it difficult to feel hope, so I knew it would be tough for them to be objective. I wanted each child to have an opportunity to express how they saw life by talking with someone who had no prior interaction with them. This cross-parenting experience allowed each child to talk about themselves without being interrupted with statements like: "Tell the truth, That's not what I'm seeing." or "Really?" In other words, to share their deepest feelings with someone who wouldn't give them toxic feedback.

The first questionnaire asked them to select all the things they liked to do – sports, reading, building blocks, and games. The second questionnaire asked about their academic issues – late or missed homework, forgetfulness, and organization. The third questionnaire asked about their behavioral outcomes in given situations – angry outbursts, using blame or excuses, and interrupting.

Most parents enjoyed going through the questionnaires and hearing all the wonderful things other children liked. They saw many similarities in the strengths and challenges of their own child. But there was always the parent who tried to eavesdrop on their own child's conversation. I explained to the parents that they should focus on the child they were with and not worry about how their own child was answering the questions.

"Remember," I said lightheartedly, "Make sure you focus on the child you're with or I'll have to come by and discipline you."

They all chuckled because they knew the temptation was great.

And it was.

I remember a dad who couldn't resist listening to his son Damon's responses. Dad was leaning back in his chair trying to hear what Damon was saying. I walked over and stood between him and Damon. With a smile I pointed and said, "I think the child you are questioning is over there."

"I just wanted to make sure he answered them the right way."

Damon's dad laughed as he leaned back in to focus on the child he was with.

When the exercise was over, the parents went into a break-out session and heard great things about their child, things they could no longer see or had forgotten about. They were amazed at how talkative their child was and how open and willing they were to talk about their concerns in school and at home. These parents learned that their own perceptions had greatly changed from happiness for their child to skepticism about their future. It was validation that perhaps they needed a different approach to work at building self-worth.

These two-day workshops were always fun. And, I never met an unkind person. Even though parents came to the workshop wearing the face of someone who felt hopeless, they left with a much more hopeful outlook. I made sure that before I started each workshop, I recited the Prayer of St. Francis to myself. It seemed to put me in the right frame of mind to work with their frustrations.

While I was in the process of creating my two-day family workshops and six-week adult workshops, I learned the ADHD Coaches Organization was accepting requests for proposals. I sent mine in and it was accepted. I presented my first conference workshop at their second annual conference in St. Louis.

I attended other conferences and began to notice that no one seemed to speak on coaching in groups, whether it was for families or adults. I wondered if I could be accepted to present such a topic at an international conference. Doubt allowed me to push the idea aside for a while. However, the thought kept nagging at me. I started at the top and submitted a proposal to CHADD (Children and Adults with ADHD), known throughout the world.

It was rejected.

It would be three more years of rejections from CHADD before I received my acceptance letter. When my proposal was finally accepted in 2007, I was awarded the prestigious recognition of "Innovative Programs" for my six-week adult workshop.

When I arrived at the conference I was nervous because I didn't know what to expect. I stood by my table and answered attendees' questions. A psychologist came by and introduced herself. She began reading the display. Then she spoke.

"I've been concerned that coaches are doing therapy with out a license. There's a lot of psychological issues that go with ADHD and you people need to be careful what you're doing."

"Wow!" I thought. "How do I answer this?"

Then the words came.

Using the charts that were on the poster board, I explained.

"The adult groups are about education and building skills and strategies around tasks that are difficult for ADHD people to see through to completion. I'm careful not to dive into their psychological barriers to achieving success. If a barrier does become obvious, I refer them to their psychologist."

I continued to talk about how I look at the manifestations of ADHD life and do my best to teach adults how they think differently – meaning their fast and scattered thought process. She understood that my concern was about helping adults achieve their potential through skills and strategy building.

We talked a bit further and she ended our conversation with, "Well, I just wanted to let you know how some of us feel."

"Thank you, and I do understand."

I felt good about how I handled my first challenging question.

I worked hard the next year to connect with conference speakers by volunteering to help at conferences. In a of couple years, I was presenting for the ADHD Coaches Organization and the Ohio Psychological Association. It felt good to present my ideas on ADHD to two such powerful organizations.

My next goal would be to get on national television.

"I wonder if I could get on TV," I thought. *"That would be a stretch. I don't even know how you go about doing that."*

I wanted to let people know about the positive approach to managing ADHD instead of the five-second media reports that left those of us with ADHD feeling hopeless. Those messages were about what was wrong with being ADHD without any resolution or hope. Rarely did you hear about the bright, intuitive, and creative side of these people. I wanted my own segment so I could talk about the positive things professionals are doing to help those with ADHD.

To shed some light on a more positive approach, a certified professional organizer, A. J. Pfander, and I developed "Collaborative Solutions." The purpose was to bring together professionals interested in a successful outcome for a mutual client and patient with ADHD. We asked psychologist Ken DeLuca to join us in putting together a news segment on ADHD with Kathy, who was one of our clients and his patient. He agreed. We then connected with the local Sr. Health Anchor for NBC, Monica Robins, and garnered a spot on the evening news.

The television crew filmed interviews at my office and at the psychologist's office. I felt very relaxed during the interview. When they left, I was excited and couldn't wait to see the segment on the news. The evening it was scheduled to show, one of the worst lightning and rain storms rolled through. Our lights were flickering and I thought for sure that no one would get to see it. But we never lost power and the segment was on as scheduled. That segment spread around the country and people called and emailed from everywhere to ask for help.

Another area on which I wanted to make an impact was the educational system. I'd been doing two-hour workshops here and there for educators. But I wanted something stronger, more powerful. I decided to expand the two-hour workshop into a five-week workshop. This enabled attendees to practice their newly learned skills with their current ADHD students and report results back to the class.

Before working with their students they were asked to experience ADHD themselves without telling anyone what they were doing. During the day, for each person they encountered, they were to respond with one of the following:

> I don't know.
> I forgot.
> What do you mean?
> Let me think a minute.
> What meeting?
> Did you tell me to do that?
> Can you believe I forgot?
> Was that today?
> What is your name again?
> I can't believe I did that.
> I left it at home.
> I forgot my lunch.

I wanted these educators to experience first-hand the emotional and social impact a student feels when their recall fails them. Obviously it had a more powerful impact on teachers without ADHD. On the other hand, it became confirmation to some that perhaps they had ADHD.

The first time I did this 15 teachers were involved. More than half of them couldn't bring themselves to say any of the phrases above. It was too embarrassing. A few of them lasted about an hour but felt too humiliated to continue. Some even reported that it made them feel stupid to say any of those phrases. That alone was an eye opener for them.

Only one teacher lasted for four hours. She was a bright and energetic person who was not ADHD. Here is how Jean's morning went.

"Hi, Jean. See you later for the IEP meeting."

Jean quickly turned around and said, "What IEP meeting?"

"The one at 4:00 today."

"Oh, right. I'll be there."

She paused and said, "Who is it for?"

"It's for Billy," her colleague said curiously.

"Oh, that's right."

At this point Jean was just smiling to herself, knowing what she was up to. Every time someone asked her a question she followed the assignment and did a fine job sounding like a person with ADHD. She kept wondering what her peers might have been thinking.

In her classroom, Jean kept forgetting students' names and pretended to have a difficult time recalling words. She just laughed it off, but inside was beginning to feel embarrassed.

Just before the bell rang to dismiss the students, she said, "That's all for today, I'll see you tomorrow."

One of the students said, "Ms. Jean, you didn't collect our homework."

"Did I give you homework?"

She paused.

"Oh, that's right. Okay, hand it in."

All but one student was laughing. After class, Annie went up to Ms. Jean and looked at her with great concern.

"Ms. Jean, did you take your ADD medicine this morning?"

Ms. Jean just pursed her lips together.

"Thank you, Annie. I'm just a little confused today."

"I get confused, too."

The fifth grader was ADD herself and her expression of empathy for her teacher's situation was heartfelt. Now Jean was concerned. She felt she'd let her students down. More troubling to her, she felt the disappointment an ADD student feels.

Jean continued her assignment well into a morning staff meeting. She had intentionally taken 10 minutes of the meeting to just ramble on as she tried to come up with words to explain a point. She also asked colleagues to re-explain things, and pretended to have a hard time finding information for the meeting.

After the meeting, the principal pulled her aside.

"Are you okay, Jean?"

Jean couldn't go any further. She explained the class assignment to her principal. He was quite surprised. He said he didn't think she had ADHD, but knew something was wrong. He understood the exercise and was surprised at how well she pulled it off. Jean's goal was reached but the idea of someone asking her if she'd forgotten to take her ADHD medicine was something she would never forget. Annie had connected with her in an emotional way. She wanted to cry.

As a class we laughed at how well she pulled off the assignment. But when we got serious about its impact, everyone in the room agreed that if a third or fourth grader had been acting as Jean had throughout the day, most teachers would not have pulled the child aside and asked if he or she were okay. They might have assumed the student was being difficult or didn't get enough sleep, and perhaps that they were ADHD. Even though Jean was acting out of her norm, the point was that she was extended the courtesy of being asked if she was okay.

I continued this exercise in different workshops over the years. It brought in many referrals and my business grew exponentially. I was at a point where I needed help to manage the overwhelming amount of paperwork. It would take someone special with a kind heart and patience to work with me and she'd have to be able to communicate well with this population. The problem was solved sooner than I had expected.

One evening, Jim and I went out to dinner. As we were being seated, I heard a man's voice.

"Joyce! Joyce!"

I turned around and there was Jeff, from the old neighborhood. I went to his table to say hi to him and his family. Another neighbor, Margie, was also there.

"So how are you doing? How's the business going?" Jeff asked.

"I'm doing fine, but I'm looking for someone to help out a few hours a week."

Jeff and Margie immediately pointed to Jeff's wife, Carol. "She'll do it! She'd love to."

I just laughed not taking them too seriously. Jeff and Margie were always goofing around. But not this time. Two months later Carol began working for me. It took a while for me to let go and trust someone else with my baby – my business – but Carol's nursing background and personality were a perfect fit.

With Carol's assistance, I found more time to write and present. I approached the psychiatric departments at various local hospitals about doing grand rounds. Grand rounds are monthly talks provided to doctors on new products or alternative ideas for the care of their patients. The head of the department of each hospital agreed that doctors needed more help in this area and that a different perspective on ADHD would be helpful. I also needed them to know that ADHD Coaching was not therapy.

The grand rounds seemed to go well and I felt I had made an impact on getting therapists to consider that after therapy an ADHD Coach might be helpful in teaching life skills specific to their patient's needs. Again, this opened the doors for more referrals and my adult group workshops were growing.

Out of those workshops came perhaps my greatest achievement, the publication of a study on the efficacy of ADHD Coaching. It became important for me to know if the adult workshop was having an effect on the attendees long after the workshop was over. I entertained the idea of doing a study but couldn't see how that would happen.

"Me, do a study?"

I hated statistics and celebrated when I was done with the class. So, I felt certain that my doing a study on my workshop's effects on adults with ADHD wasn't likely to happen because it involved statistics. However, the seed was planted in my head.

"What if I got someone to help me with the statistical data? I could probably write the paper. But that's a lot of work and getting published is not very likely. After all, I'm not a PhD. I don't even have a Masters."

I struggled with the idea for weeks and months.

Why couldn't I get published? I owed it to myself to try. And if it didn't work out, then I'd still have learned if my workshops were effective. I started searching for academic articles on ADHD Coaching. I found it hard to believe that for as long as ADHD Coaching had been around, no one had ever researched its effectiveness.

Needless to say, my mind began racing with ideas. I looked back at the questionnaire I'd been using on the first night of the adult workshops. The questionnaire I developed measured 22 cognitive, emotional, and behavioral outcomes of living with ADHD. I wanted to know the frequency with which these 22 areas of concern affected adults prior to and after coaching.

I followed the guidelines for administering a survey. Beginning with the start of each six-week workshop, before any explanation of coaching began, I continued to collect data for four years. Every attendee signed a statement that they were willing to have their data used in a study. Still, there were many more things to be considered.

To get over the hurdle of running the statistical data, I called a few friends I knew who were statisticians and asked them to run some numbers. However, they didn't feel qualified to work on a psychology study. The Ohio Psychological Association directed me to Baldwin Wallace University where I found a professor who understood statistics for psychology. We met several times to discuss the purpose of the study and to develop the thesis. I was in awe of this person's knowledge. I could have never done it without her.

Four years and many drafts later, I submitted the study to the Journal of Attention Disorders. It had to go through a peer review and I was nervous about it being rejected. It was difficult to explain that this study was not measuring outcomes based on the diagnostic manual used by psychologists. It was measuring outcomes based on the on going concerns that ADHD Coaches and clients work on together. In 2009 the study was published online and in May, 2010, "Efficacy of ADHD Coaching for Adults with ADHD" was published in the *Journal of Attention Disorders*.

ABSTRACT

This is perhaps the first study on the efficacy of ADHD Coaching for adults with ADHD (Adults) and its long-term effect. Forty-five adults (30 females, 15 males) rated 22 Areas of Concern (AOC) before and after the coaching experience. Factor analysis of the 22 AOC items revealed five AOC factors. Descriptive statistics and inter-correlations were analyzed on the five AOC factors. Test-retest reliabilities for each factor ranged from .44 to .61, all statistically significant at the $p < .01$ level of significance. Additionally, there are many significant correlations between factors at similar times and factors at the different time periods, demonstrating the efficacy of ADHD Coaching. Repeated measures two-way Analysis of Variance was used to determine the effects of ADHD Coaching alone, as well as the combined effect with therapy or stimulants. Results indicate that ADHD Coaching is having the desired effect on the AOC factors.

The positive outcome of this study, gave ADHD Coaching the recognition it deserved. It opened the door for others to consider further studies or to replicate this one. I was proud to be the first one to step up and make it happen. After this, I never questioned my ability to complete what I set out to do – no matter how challenging!

There were a number of coaches within the ACO who talked about working with college students. It made me think back to graduation day when the President stated that I wanted to help those with ADHD. I felt it was time to fulfill that desire. Eight years after graduating from Lorain County Community College, I fulfilled a long-held dream to give back to the college for all the years they helped me earn my degree. I developed a special Introduction to College course specifically for students with Attention Deficit Disorder. After a couple of pilot courses, funded through grants written by the Office of Special Needs Services, I was introduced to the Department for Student Development where I was challenged to integrate ADHD Coaching into the curriculum for the Fall 2011 school year. I met the challenge and was excited to have returned to my alma mater to help students succeed in college the first time, not the third or fourth.

I was now teaching, something my mother had told me to do 40 years earlier. As I looked into the eyes of those first-year college students on their first day of class, I saw hopelessness and frustration. I felt their pain when they'd say, "I understand what I have to do. It's making it happen that's the problem."

The frustration in their voices was familiar to me and I couldn't help but see those first nine ADHD boys I had taught 12 years earlier.

I had my work cut out for me and I was anxious to get started. One thing I knew for sure was that these students would be fighters. They wouldn't be sitting in my class if they didn't have even the tiniest amount of hope.

Each semester started with a discussion on living with ADHD. We talked about how it affected their past, present, and future. Students spoke freely about their high school years and how they felt unprepared for college. They came from the poorest to the wealthiest school districts. They said that teachers, and sometimes parents, simply "gave up on me and just passed me through to get rid of me." They felt their teachers either couldn't teach them or just didn't care. The tone of voice of these college freshmen reflected their anger and frustration with the education system. I described my experiences with college and assured them that, like me, they could earn a degree. They just needed to understand their own thought process and decide if they would let it help them or continue to hinder them. Then we talked about strategies to help them overcome the difficult times.

The majority of these students could not write a complete sentence. They didn't capitalize sentences or put periods at the end. It was as if they removed the shift key and the period key from the keyboard. Their work reflected their lack of pride. It reflected an I-don't-care attitude, while I knew deep down inside they did care. Their writing and spelling skills were nowhere near high school level, let alone college. Their college years would be made more difficult by systems that just passed them through their elementary, middle school, and high school years. Sadly, students knew it was happening, but didn't care because they were anxious to "get out of there." They knew they weren't stupid, they just wanted another chance and hoped college would give it to them.

As they discovered more about themselves through observation, they found it easier to use the new strategies they were learning. Each new skill left them feeling more hopeful and their voices expressed a much stronger self-esteem. As the semester rolled on, they became a family. They learned to appreciate their ADHD while understanding they had a lot of catching up to do in terms of managing it. But, they were willing. I looked forward to each semester, knowing how much of an impact I could have on these students and their future. They were truly grateful for a course designed for students like them.

I loved my work and had no complaints, except that I needed time to do more!

One day I received a phone call from a company called A Working Mind. They wanted to talk about Cogmed Working Memory Training, a program marketed to people who struggle with attention or focus issues. The training itself is designed to improve one's cognitive focus and attention functions. As a coach, I would provide support and weekly feedback on the client's progress.

One of the criteria to become a Certified Cogmed Coach was to take the training myself. I found it to be quite challenging and at times frustrating. Having to remember sequences of numbers or letters was difficult especially when they were shifting or rotating. Sometimes lights would flash on a grid and you had to use the mouse to click and repeat the exact sequence.

It wasn't until a month or two after the training was complete that I started to recognize the change in my thinking. I was relaxing in my favorite chair one evening. An off-task thought just popped in my head totally unrelated to what I was doing. Normally, I would have gotten up and taken care of the distracting thought and then forgotten to go back to my initial task. This time I didn't do that. I just reached over and wrote down the distraction to deal with it another time.

A couple minutes later I said out loud, "What just happened? I didn't jump up and do what I was thinking! Wow, that's a first."

Then I remembered Cogmed.

"Could it be the training?"

This type of change continued to occur for at least a year. It was obvious that the long-term effects helped to develop my working memory. I was taking more time to think about things before I did them, and although I'm still ADHD and will always be, there is greater ease in my recall and task completion.

With so many things coming together for me, I was ready to tackle my life-long goal: writing my memoirs. It was time to tell my story and help others like me recognize when they needed help and to help children feel better about themselves at a much earlier age. But I was a bit intimidated about the sensitivity of the stories. While I knew I would eventually write my book, it took me nearly ten years to feel ready.

In 2004 I did research to see if someone had ever written a book about ADHD as a life story. I didn't find anything. Encouraged, I started gathering my information and developing chapter ideas for my own book. A story line had started to evolve. I got serious about my writing and began the process of putting words on paper. I wasn't sure how good my writing was, so I sent a few chapters to friends for an opinion. To my surprise, everyone's response was "It sounds like a speech."

Of course it did! That's all I'd been doing for the past ten years.

I came to realize that I needed formal training on writing a memoir. So I took a writing course online through *Writer's Market*. Then, I sought the help of a writing coach and wrote the first draft. The problem was having to steal time to write from the time I was already committed to spending on my work, family, and home. I found much of my inspiration for writing at the park on Lake Erie, or in the quiet writing nook I set up at home. It was cathartic in many ways and I found the whole experience of writing a book to be quite satisfying.

I feel blessed to have learned so many ways to help people with ADHD. My years of having coached children, college students, and adults has clearly taught me that the earlier we reach people with ADHD, the less likely they are to have so much anger and frustration.

Learning to manage your ADHD as a child becomes a natural process, like picking up a video game and figuring it out with little instructions.

Learning to manage your ADHD as a college student creates a lot of anger and resentment and anger over the many years they spent feeling misunderstood. College students with ADHD often feel that everyone has given up on them, yet they haven't given up on themselves.

And when learning to manage ADHD as an adult, suppressed emotions return. ADHD adults become very frustrated about their many missed opportunities. They have been left with many bridges to mend and are overwhelmed as to where to start.

MY LIFE'S JOURNEY, as difficult as it was at times, showed me an inner strength I didn't know I had. Understanding how my brain works and accepting the rules I needed to live by was crucial to all of my achievements. I follow those rules most of the time, but it would be a boring life to follow them all of the time. I love to take an occasional day here and there and just be ADHD.

After all, it is my nature to just go with the flow.

A family of graduates, 2005.

chapter thirteen

Epilogue

"For if you suffer your people to be ill-educated, and their manners to be corrupted from their infancy, and then punish them for those crimes to which their first education disposed them, what else is to be concluded from it, but that you first make thieves and then punish them?"

Utopia
Sir Thomas More (1516)

I FIRST HEARD MORE'S QUOTE in 1998 when Drew Barrymore played the lead character, Danielle, in *Ever After: A Cinderella Story*. She was speaking to the Prince, using More's quote in an effort to rescue a servant. She questioned how someone could punish a person who, from their infancy, was poorly educated and had never learned proper manners. It felt to her that people were being punished for doing what they were taught to do. No matter what a person's heart said about right or wrong, they had to dismiss it as "not correct behavior."

As a child I was corrected when I approached things in a way that made sense to me. Inevitably, I would be corrected and shown the right way. When I did it the right way, it was clumsy and didn't feel natural. To my parents, it appeared I was trying to be difficult. Eventually I would rebel because I believed my way was better and easier. It was very frustrating to try to conform.

Many people live through a childhood filled with anger and frustrations, much as I did. They may have great assets to offer the world but at a very young age they are locked into believing that they only have deficits. Like the people referred to in Sir Thomas More's quote, I came to believe that my life was supposed to be difficult, and despite whatever potential I had, I felt certain I would never be allowed to live up to it. I felt trapped.

As children we can't understand the workings of the mind and we certainly can't understand that people have negative childhood experiences that emerge later in life. That could have been the problem in my relationship with my dad. I couldn't understand why he imposed restrictions on me and then expected me to just obey as the others did. I was too curious to simply conform and to him that was disrespectful. Had my parents understood that minds work differently, they could have been more accepting of my differences.

When the parents of 9-year-old Patrick saw the visual of the Bridge, it was an epiphany – they finally began to understand what Patrick's brain felt like to him. Before that moment, they didn't have enough knowledge to understand what Patrick truly meant when he said he was confused. They had been as frustrated as Patrick was. But now they had a much clearer understanding. And Patrick no longer felt his parents were choosing not to understand him. They simply didn't know.

The process of parenting can make you feel as if you're a failure, with fingers pointing at you from every direction, pointing out your shortcomings. Like many parents, I couldn't get my children to do what I asked. My inability to get results told me I was failing as a parent. And, just as my parents felt I was being disrespectful to them, I felt my children were being disrespectful to me. I was simply following in my parent's footsteps.

There was a missing piece in the puzzle of my life and many times I kept thinking that something was wrong with me. I could never put my finger on it. But as I got closer to understanding how ADHD was affecting my life, I saw things in me that I didn't like. I had much to learn, and education became the missing piece.

In the process of putting all the pieces of the puzzle together I was both devastated and elated. The devastation came from learning that my ADHD was damaging my personal relationships. As I reflect on that today, I find it incomprehensible. It's amazing how the mind can be so distracted and so involved that it cannot see the obvious. Since "distracted" was my norm, it's no wonder people saw me as a scatterbrain.

The elation came from learning that I could change those relationships. It meant there was hope for a much brighter future than I ever could have imagined.

Not everything about ADHD is negative. There were plenty of times when my ideas were labeled as insightful or brilliant. When that happened at work, I expected to have my ideas implemented – within a week! In offices things don't happen like they do in your own business, where you are the boss and decision maker. There are reviews, approvals, and hoops to jump through. I had to learn to slow down and wait for the process to evolve. I found that very difficult. I also had to learn that strongly expressing my opinion did nothing positive for how I was perceived.

Even though I survived working in offices, my guard was always up. Every day I fought the internal battle of controlling my impulsivity. My self-esteem was up and down constantly. All too often, I felt less effective than everyone else.

I often think of the young lady in my office who walked up to me all crouched down so no one would see her. I imagine she, too, had much to offer and perhaps lacked the patience to wait for the right time to make her point. Looking back, it was clear she wasn't getting the right kind of help. What she needed was an ADHD Coach; or at the very least a job coach. I still think about her today and how helpless she must have felt. It doesn't seem right that anyone should have to worry about their job just because they have ADHD. Unfortunately, her story makes me hesitant to advise anyone to disclose their ADHD. And there are more people like her out there.

I never used to talk about disclosure until the fourth week of a workshop, when I explain the possible risks of telling other people you have ADHD. During the first weeks of training, clients become much more positive about their lives. They are excited to learn there is a relationship between their ADHD and why they are late, why they don't complete things on time, and why they are unable to keep their emotions under control. By telling their boss what they've learned, they hope it will help their somewhat difficult job situation and all will be well. What happens far too often, however, is that their bosses use this new-found information against them and eventually they are let go. I felt so bad after a third person told this to me that I changed my presentation. I now explain in the first week the risks and possible outcomes of disclosing their ADHD before they have learned the appropriate methods and systems to use to manage their challenges effectively. When those methods and systems are in place, disclosure becomes an option and may not be necessary.

I'VE MET SOME INCREDIBLE SOULS through my coaching business. One, in particular, stands out because his story was so like mine. John attended the workshop when he was about 40. When I asked the group if they had difficulty reading, John said, "I haven't read a book in years. Not because I don't have the time, but what happens is, when I read I'll get to chapter three and can't recall anything from chapters one and two. It's just so frustrating."

Nearly everyone in the class agreed with John's experience.

There is no doubt that reading is difficult for this population. I know from my own experience that unless I do something to keep my thoughts from wandering, I'll just give up.

I work with my clients to teach them how to read as a person with ADHD. It requires active reading. That means every few paragraphs or so, jotting down a character's name, a location, or just the first few words of the paragraph. Doing this takes you away from any wandering thoughts and returns your focus back to the text. As you continue to do this, eventually you become fully engaged in the story with a better chance of enjoying the pleasure of reading a book to completion.

Several months after John attended the ADHD workshop, I ran across him at a car dealership. He was sitting there calmly reading a book. I said hello and he began to tell me how well he was doing. When he began talking about how much he enjoyed reading, he had tears in his eyes. He said his wife couldn't get over how much he read day after day. Then he added, "I'm an avid reader now. And, I'm so grateful to you."

That meant a lot to me and I was overjoyed for him.

Imagine how college students feel when they have so much reading to do and they, too, face the same problem of their minds wandering. Students tell me they didn't read much of anything throughout high school. Their comment is always "what's the point? I'll forget anyway." I'm sad for them because, like me, deep down inside so many of them really do want to read. Most believe that the high school issues they experienced are in the past and college is the opportunity for a fresh start. They don't realize that their issues in high school are simply carried over into college. They still think the school, the teacher, or anything else was largely responsible for their failures.

I ask them not to give up on reading or college for that matter, because there is so much to learn about the effects ADHD has had on their lives. What they are embarking upon is a journey that will forever change their lives.

Still, some are not quite sure why they have to be in a special college strategy class. The following quote is from one of those angry and upset students.

> On the first day of College 102, I was pretty irritated that I had to be in a class explaining about ADD/ADHD and how to overcome that in a college setting. I felt like I knew everything I needed to know to get through and graduate from college. But as I kept attending this class, I realized how wrong I was that I thought I knew everything to get through college. My college 102 class taught me more than I already knew about myself and ADD.

It's that same attitude that carried me through college. There was always that drive to succeed and to prove to myself that I had what it takes to graduate from college. My will to live and thrive gave me the strength I needed to succeed, but at the same time, I feared success.

More specifically, what I feared was the unknown.

With each new business adventure, I wondered how I would ever pull it off. But I never doubted my ability and I always kept my faith that God would be there to guide me and give me the strength I needed to keep moving forward. I just got up every day and did what I felt was right. I had to dismiss my fears of failing and just let life happen. And happen it did!

One year, at a conference for ADHD Coaches, a colleague of mine and I were talking about these fears. It seemed silly to hear myself talk about feeling inadequate. It made me realize I was still being controlled by my past fears of failure. Those fears should have been behind me, many years ago. As we spoke, Kat remembered a quote by Marianne Williamson in *A Return To Love* and asked me to read it. I did, and instantly felt the power behind it. I keep it posted in my office and read it often to remind myself of the powerful person I am.

> Our deepest fear is not that we are inadequate. Our deepest fear is that we are powerful beyond measure. It is our light, not our darkness that most frightens us. We ask ourselves, Who am I to be brilliant, gorgeous, talented, fabulous? Actually, who are you not to be? You are a child of God. Your playing small does not serve the world. There is nothing enlightened about shrinking so that other people won't feel insecure around you. We are all meant to shine, as children do. We were born to make manifest the glory of God that is within us. It's not just in some of us; it's in everyone. And as we let our own light shine, we unconsciously give other people permission to do the same. As we are liberated from our own fear, our presence automatically liberates others.

There were many bright spots in my life that also kept me moving forward. Most of them I was unable to appreciate until now. They were events and voices of encouragement and gratefulness.

Sr. Mary Ferdinand wrote, ". . . keep on making sacrifices and keep smiling when things go wrong." (1963)

My best friend, Jane, gave me the book *Courage is Contagious* and wrote in it, "To my very courageous friend. Live your dream." (1998)

I remember the special Mother's Day gift from my children. They put together a scrapbook of articles I'd written, awards I'd won, and photos of the many civic responsibilities I'd taken on. It was a reminder of the wonderful life I had. All I could do was cry.

Throughout my college years and well into the building of my business, my family sent me notes of encouragement. I would send them updates on my achievements and they'd write back.

"Mom, we're so happy for you. We appreciated how you fight for what you believe in and that you try to do what is best for people."

Their enthusiasm and encouragement were infectious. And they still are.

With the help and support of my family, friends, and colleagues, and my indomitable will to succeed, I have moved on from those years when my parents and teachers told me what was right for me, how to act, and how to react. Back then they looked at my behavior as that of a rebellious child and not as that of a person whose brain simply thought about life in a different way. They believed they knew what was best for me. I knew otherwise. Their care was stifling and I needed the freedom to be myself.

Once I was able to take ownership of who I am, a woman with ADHD, the journey to embrace my life began. I had learned to turn my greatest deficit into my greatest asset.

bibliography

Jones, Clare (no date). *ADDitude Magazine*. What is slow processing speed? [online], Available: http://www.additudemag.com/q%26a/ask_the_learning_expert/1553.html. retrieved 1/7/2012).

Anderson, Robert (1996). I Never Sang for My Father. New York: Dramatists Guild.

Kubik, J. A. (2010, March). Efficacy of ADHD Coaching for adults with ADHD. Journal of Attention Disorders.
http://www.sagepub.com/journals.nav

Solden, Sari (1998). Women with Attention Deficit Disorder. Grass Valley, CA: Underwood Books.

More, Thomas, Sir (1992). Utopia. New York: Alfred A. Knopf.

Weathers, L., Ph.D. (2013). The role of dopamine. [online], Available: http://www.adhdtreatment.org/adhd-child/180-the-real-non-defective-neurology-of-adhd.html retrieved 1/7/2012.

Williamson, Marianne (1992). A Return to Love: Reflections on the Principles of A Course in Miracles. New York, NY: HarperPerennial/ Harper Collins Publishers

resources

ADDitude Magazine.
www.additudemag.com (p.103)

ADHD Coaches Organization.
www.adhdcoaches.org (p.125, 140)

Adult Children of Alcoholics World Service
Organization. www.adultchildren.org (p.34)

American Coaching Association
www.americoach.org (p.113, 143)

Attention Deficit Disorder Association
(ADDA). www.add.org (p.65)

Avon Lake Junior Women's Club (Women's Club of Avon Lake). Avon Lake OH
www.avon-oh.patch.com/events/womens-club-of-avon-lake-meeting (p.44, 125)

A Working Mind, Middleburg Hts. OH.
www.aworkingmind.com/wp/ (p.152)

Bridge To Success Skills Training, LLC, Avon Lake OH.
www.bridgetosuccess.net (p.113)

CHADD (Children and Adults with Attention Deficit Disorder)
www.chadd.org (p.142)

Cleveland State University, Cleveland OH.
http://csuohio.edu (p.101)

Cogmed Working Memory Training, http://www.cogmed.com (p.152)

Cuyahoga Community College, Cleveland OH
http://www.tri-c.edu/ (p.119, 124)

General Federation of Women's Clubs, GWC@gfwc.org (p.44, 125)

Ken DeLuca & Associates, North Ridgeville OH.
www.kendelucainc.org (p.144)

Lorain County Community College, ElyriaOH.
www.lorainccc.edu (p.91, 151)

Manos, Michael, PhD. Head, Center for Pediatric Behavioral Health, Pediatric Institute, Cleveland Clinic, Cleveland OH. www.clevelandclinic.org (p.82)

Ohio Psychological Association (OPA). www.ohpsych.org (p.143)

The Press, Avon Lake OH
http://2presspapers.northcoastnow.com (p.140)

Robins, Monica, Sr. Health Anchor, NBC (WKYC-TV)
Cleveland OH, www.wkyc.com/company/bios/robins.aspx (p.144)

Toastmasters, www.toastmasters.org (p.113)

Writer's Market, www.writersmarket.com (p.154)

about the author

JOYCE A. KUBIK, CMC, IS AN internationally recognized ADHD coach, Certified Master Coach, and skills trainer. Founder and President of Bridge to  Success, she is the author of four books that aid in the management of ADHD, including Plan For Success, used by elementary, secondary, and college/university students. In several schools, such as Harvard University and Landmark College, Plan for Success is used as a learning and performance-enhancement tool in classes for students with ADHD. She has also been published in the national periodical "ADDitude

Magazine" and many local newspapers. Kubik has presented at several hospital and pediatric grand rounds for Continuing Medical Education, including The Cleveland Clinic. She has also developed and presents workshops for children, families, and adults affected by ADHD. Joyce has given presentations and keynote addresses at schools, education centers, colleges, NAMI, Kiwanis International, and NASA.

Her adult workshops became the basis for the ground-breaking and award-winning research study, "Efficacy of ADHD Coaching for Adults with ADHD" (JAD 2010). Joyce Kubik has been recognized by the Ohio Psychological Association and the International Association of Coaches for her pioneering study. Her work has led her to train life coaches internationally.

Kubik is a member of these organizations related to ADHD:

CHADD | Children and Adults with ADHD
     Support group coordinator
ADHD | Coaches Organization.
     Board member , Conference chair for 2013.
ADDA | Attention Deficit Disorder for Adults
CPA | Cleveland Psychological Association
OPA | Ohio Psychological Association
ACA | American Coaching Association
IAC | International Association of Coaches

Joyce Kubik has appeared nationally on ABC, local cable stations; developed videos for reaching college students; and designed and developed a specialized introduction to college courses she teaches to first year ADHD students at a local college to keep them in school. She is also a Certified Working Memory Coach for Cogmed Working Memory Training.

440-933-8309
Kubikja@bridgetosuccess.net
www.bridgetosuccess.net

Ceremony honors LCCC grads

Rob Phillips
The Chronicle-Telegram

More than 1,000 students earn degrees

A dream realized

LCCC grad overcomes disorder

Dave Perozek
The Chronicle-Telegram

ELYRIA — Frustration, anger and depression used to be a way of life for Avon Lake resident Joyce Kubik.

Kubik waged a daily struggle with her own mind, which would constantly race from one subject to another, never allowing her to focus.

At Lorain County Community College's commencement on

Saturday, she did something many people told her she'd never do: She received a college degree.

It wasn't until eight years ago that Kubik, now 54, discovered a name for her ailment.

"They had a thing on (the television program) '20/20' about a guy who had attention deficit disorder," Kubik said. "My husband and I looked at each other

See DREAM, A6

GRADUATION AT LAST: Joyce Kubik, who has struggled with ADHD, graduated Saturday from LCCC.

GENE KREBS / CHRONICLE

DREAM

From **A1**

and said, 'That's it.' "

Kubik visited her doctor and told her about what she saw on television. It made sense. The doctor finally diagnosed Kubik with attention deficit hyperactivity disorder at the age of 46.

Ever since, Kubik has dedicated her life to helping herself and helping others with ADHD.

On Saturday, she received an associate of arts in psychology from LCCC. She plans to get her bachelor's degree in psychology from Cleveland State University next year.

But it's the degree from LCCC that will matter more to her, she said.

"I feel so good about this associate's degree," she said. "I never thought I'd get to this point. If you had ADD, you'd understand the emotions of getting that degree. Everybody would tell me I would never finish college."

In fact, before her diagnosis, Kubik tried college twice at Cuyahoga Community College but failed both times.

Kubik now runs her own business called Bridges to Success, coaching families of and individuals with ADD and ADHD. She also maintains a busy speaking schedule. Earlier this month, she spoke at the ADHD annual conference in Chicago.

ADD affects a person's ability to concentrate. Adding the hyperactivity part means not only that the mind is constantly moving but the body is also. That makes it difficult to learn.

Medication can help, but people with ADD or ADHD usually need more than that. Kubik said they must learn how to manage a constantly shifting mind.

"If you haven't learned to manage the confusion in your head, then you can't manage anything," she said.

Kubik began her pursuit of a degree from LCCC in 1996, taking

two to three classes per semester while running her business.

Her first class was a public speaking course that met each Saturday morning.

Kubik made her husband swear not to tell their three teenage children about the classes she was taking. The children thought she was out doing women's club work those days.

Kubik didn't let her kids know about it until she posted her first "A" on the refrigerator door.

"They couldn't believe I would hide that from them," she said.

Kubik's graduation is not the only one in the family this year. Her 21-year-old daughter Jennifer — who also has ADHD — will graduate from Ohio State University on June 14.

"Only Jennifer and I realize what an honor this is," Kubik said about graduation. "It's very emotional."

Contact Dave Perozek at dperozek@chronicletelegram.com or 329-7119.

May 18, 2002 - LCCC/CSU
Associates of Arts - Psychology

The Elyria Chronicle-Telegram, 2002.